IN ALL MY WAYS

*Essays on Encountering God
In Every Day Life*

AMY MAHAN ROBBINS

WESTBOW
PRESS®
A DIVISION OF THOMAS NELSON
& ZONDERVAN

This book is a work of non-fiction. Unless otherwise noted, the author
and the publisher make no explicit guarantees as to the accuracy of
the information contained in this book and in some cases, names of
people and places have been altered to protect their privacy.

WestBow Press books may be ordered through booksellers or by contacting:

WestBow Press
A Division of Thomas Nelson & Zondervan
1663 Liberty Drive
Bloomington, IN 47403
www.westbowpress.com
844-714-3454

Because of the dynamic nature of the Internet, any web addresses or
links contained in this book may have changed since publication and
may no longer be valid. The views expressed in this work are solely those
of the author and do not necessarily reflect the views of the publisher,
and the publisher hereby disclaims any responsibility for them.

Any people depicted in stock imagery provided by Getty Images are
models, and such images are being used for illustrative purposes only.
Certain stock imagery © Getty Images.

Scripture quotations taken from The Holy Bible, New International
Version® NIV® Copyright © 1973 1978 1984 2011 by Biblica, Inc.
TM. Used by permission. All rights reserved worldwide.

Scripture taken from the Amplified Bible, Copyright © 1954, 1958, 1962,
1964, 1965, 1987 by The Lockman Foundation. Used with permission.

ISBN: 978-1-6642-2370-7 (sc)
ISBN: 978-1-6642-2371-4 (hc)
ISBN: 978-1-6642-2372-1 (e)

Library of Congress Control Number: 2021902873

Print information available on the last page.

WestBow Press rev. date: 04/14/2021

Contents

Preface

> When God guides people, God does not hand them
> a clearly marked road map instructing them to turn
> here, to take this exit, to follow this street. God
> says, "Follow this cloud." What is it like to follow a
> cloud? A cloud on the ground is fog.[1]

I grew up on the central coast of California, in a small farming town where the coastal fog came daily and draped itself over everything like a white, wooly blanket. Heavy mist shrouded dairy, with the red metal barn filled with the echoes of mooing cows at the end of the valley, and then eased through the gaps of the hills, like slow-moving water. It slipped over the tops of small green hills and plunged down long ravines, weaving in and out of the little paddocks and oblivious to the wooden fences that separated them.

As a young girl, I loved to roam the land surrounding our house, filled with a patchwork of thick green pastures, cattle paths, and knots of live oaks. Every afternoon, just before the sun would slide beyond the rolling hills in the west, I left my room and found myself in a pasture, or a small valley, or in a gap between some low-lying hills. It did not seem to matter where I waited, now that I think about it; it always found me.

The fog.

I was fascinated by the fog, mesmerized by the way it moved and eased its way across everything. It felt magical, somehow. Each afternoon I would walk, slowly at first, convinced that I could race it, or at best keep up with it. Perhaps I could even figure out its comings and goings. But the fog always seemed to have a plan that I was not privy to. First, it was not at all predictable. The only pattern I was ever to determine about it was that it appeared late in the afternoon and went away as the sun grew higher and warmer in the sky the following day.

The cow path made an unexpected turn and suddenly dropped down to another paddock below a ridge. I picked up speed, trotting along to keep up with the changes. Soon I was out in the open, dashing through a flat expanse of pasture strewn with live oaks and scrub brush. The fog slid to either side of me, and I did not have to look back to know it was about to overtake me. The oaks surrounding me had changed, the fog dressing them in wisps and swirls the consistency of saggy, old rags. That was the thing about fog: it seemed to create change wherever it went. One by one, it reshaped the trees around me and dimmed the path in front of me. Everything familiar seemed suddenly different. I was disoriented for a time, and I stopped in the middle of what I thought was a familiar paddock. The fog had slowed and then stopped moving. It seemed heavier, more solid. It closed in on me at last and drenched my face and hair in cool dampness. The familiar path that should have been there had vanished. I was lost.

It was always like this. I had to sit and wait. The fog had its own tempo and revealed what it wanted to, when it wanted to. I could not rush it or force it to move. There are no shortcuts to take around it, nor could this process be sidestepped. I had to rest and wait. A sudden, slight breeze drifted over, and the fog lifted enough that I could see a small path nearby. I knew this path; it would lead me away from the deeply rutted cow path and up an uneven hill. I scrabbled up to the top of the hill laden with ice plant and was met with a familiar sight: home. Once inside, I made my way down the hallway to my bedroom and peered out through my window. The fog had followed and had overwhelmed everything in its path. The sky, the trees, and the little path had all vanished. The low-lying sun, which sat within the curtain of fog, gave a final, faint glow and then was gone for another day.

Today, I can no longer walk those little fields, except in my mind. Change has come. The acres and acres of velvety green paddocks have been filled in with large homes, shopping centers, medical parks, and eateries. The dairy with all its mooing cows is gone as well, along with the wooden fences with their broken-over gates. The rutted paths have been paved over by tons of concrete and slathered with tar. As I wandered those little fields, soaked by the fog, as a young girl, I did not think about grace. I don't think I knew what it was. When someone described grace to me for the first time, I had a feeling I had met it before. In time, I discovered that those runs, those races with the fog, would come to be my first, fledgling steps into His grace, and into the things of God.

Grace seems to come more quickly when the need is most desperate, and so quietly that I must remain quite still as it speaks comfort and direction into my life. When I have lost my way, or become dismayed at my own irregular walk with Him, grace has had to remind me that spiritual growth does not occur overnight. I must grow into Him, and that growth never ends while I live here on the Earth. Growth can be painful, and the writing of His messages on my heart and in my mind can seem so slow. It is not because God writes slowly; it is because the lessons I need to know are eternal. The changes in my desires, my will, my emotions, and my motivations are to be just as eternal—those are the only changes that last.

Grace, like fog, has a habit of shaping itself to whatever it comes to, masking, exposing, and sometimes blurring the edges of what we may be experiencing. The path through may not be clear. Yet in the fog, with less distraction to take our attention away from Him, His voice becomes clearer, crisper somehow. I hear; then I move. Grace has always propelled me forward, bidding me to chase it, granting favor to me I do not deserve, to a destination God has for me, on a path known only by Him. It is a grounding force that settles me and gives me a power to accomplish any task He sets before me.

Nowhere do I feel His grace more than when I am writing. When I share my own testimony and my experiences, I am also sharing my heart. Not another's. I have always kept in mind when I write that I cannot tell another person's story as well as I can my own. And though I pray that you glean some wisdom from what I share with you, it is far more important to me that you understand what the Lord has done, and is doing, for *you*. Whether they be footpaths, stepping-stones, rutted old cow trails, dusty roads, or passages through the deepest of ravines of despair, He has promised to be with us, to guide and direct us. There is a scripture in Proverbs that has always seemed to me to be the best road map for direction in life:

> Trust in the LORD with all your heart and lean not on your own understanding; in all your ways submit to him, and he will make your paths straight. (Proverbs 3:5–6 NIV)

1

Hannibal

> God is ready to help. He has everything in
> preparation before our needs begin. He has laid in
> supplies for all our wants. Before our prayers are
> presented, he has prepared his answers to them;
> blessed be his name! ... The spiritual man is a
> privileged man.[1]

When my Sunday school teacher, Mr. Hancock, described God to
us, I grasped it about as well as any child could. It was difficult for
me to imagine that anyone could be everywhere, hold up heaven and
earth in one hand, catch a falling sparrow in another, never sleep,
and yet be ever mindful to hear every prayer anyone prayed. Every
prayer. I believed it simply because he said so. And then there were
the stories—stories of missionaries visited by warring angels who
appeared at just the right time, when all hope was lost, and rescued
them from heathen tribes who did not know God at all.

Mr. Hancock would always quote from the book of Kings. I
especially liked this story. There was a king who was going to invade
Israel and take it over. The king's army surrounded the Israelite
camp, and the servant of Elisha, the prophet, was frightened. He
told the prophet about the army, and Elisha told him not to be afraid
because the army that was with them was bigger than the one that

was with their enemy. Elisha saw that the servant was still afraid, so he prayed that God would open his eyes so he could see the army. And when the servant saw it, he saw a mountain full of horses and chariots.[2]

Mr. Hancock told us about men who smuggled Bibles into countries where God was hated and how they had passed right through checkpoints as if they were invisible.

"No one stopped them! It was just like they were invisible!" Mr. Hancock would say, his eyes wide with excitement at the joy of telling the story. I was filled with wonder and interest in God, but I had no such experiences.

That is, until I met Hannibal.

I was in third grade when I first saw him. I rode the old yellow school bus to school and back each day. Each afternoon, as the bus crested the hill, my eyes began to scan the road. I was searching for him, and my heart began to pound so loudly I was sure everyone on the bus could hear it.

Thump, thump. Thump, thump. Thump, thump.

He's coming ... he's coming ... for you.

Hannibal had black eyes that seemed to scan my very soul when he would look at me. As soon as I left the safety of the school bus, he would begin to follow close behind me. Then, in a frenzy, and at a time of his own choosing, he would come after me. But just before he could get close enough, my feet would somehow manage to move, and I would run.

This scenario repeated itself every school day, week in and week out, month after month. Each day, the gut-wrenching feeling would return as I left the bus, passing only when I had placed a quarter mile between myself and Hannibal.

"Oh, for heaven's sake, he's just a chicken," my mother would say when I arrived home breathless from running. I was not consoled.

Well, she was right. Hannibal was a chicken. A fighting rooster, to be more specific. He was covered in sleek white feathers all the way up to the crest of his head, where his feathers changed to a

2

topknot that looked like a nebulous white crown. These feathers fell forward over black, bottomless eyes. Holding up this mass of quivering plumage was a pair of black, spindly legs. At the base of each leg was a gleaming yellow spur about an inch and a half long. We never knew where he had come from, only that he belonged to the neighbors who lived up the hill.

Late fall had come, and with it an invitation to join the grade school band. It had already been agreed upon that I would not be taking the tuba as an instrument, as it was much too heavy and larger than I was. So I chose a half-sized violin. I came home one afternoon with it in a black leather case. I couldn't wait to take it out, tighten and rosin the bowstrings, and practice. And then my heart sank; Hannibal would be waiting.

The bus crested the hill, air brakes puffing tiredly, and with the flip of the lever, the door swung wide to let me out. The bus disappeared down the hill, and I was alone with Hannibal again. Hannibal fluffed himself up until he was several times his usual size. Almost rhythmically, he matched my pace stride for stride as I walked. But then he did something I had not expected: he quickened his pace until he was ahead of me, cutting me off from the road that led home. He turned, appraising me for a second. Then, like a fast-pitched feathered baseball, he propelled himself through the air toward me. Something was wrong this time; my feet refused to move. I was frozen in fear.

I cannot—even now—tell you why Mr. Hancock's voice came into my head. In that instant before my sure and certain destruction, all Mr. Hancock's stories passed through my mind, all at once. Whizzing through my mind came the missionaries, their warring angels by their sides, protecting them. Following the missionaries came the Bible smugglers, passing through their dangerous checkpoints unhurt and unseen in a Godless land. My last thought was quiet, somehow. In a slow and measured voice, I heard Mr. Hancock reminding me that God was everywhere and heard every prayer we prayed to Him. What was that scripture we had memorized for the past two Sundays?

> Since ancient times no one has heard, no ear has perceived, no eye has seen any God besides you, who acts on behalf of those who wait for him. (Isaiah 64:4 NIV)

As Hannibal raced toward me, spurs raised, I realized I had never asked God to help me. I closed my eyes ...

Whack!

The prayer had barely gone from my racing heart to my mouth when my black violin case met the wild, feathered sphere that had hurled toward me. The force of the blow as feathers met leather pushed me backward and onto the gravel road. Hannibal hit the side of the case, bounced, and landed on the ground some distance away in a pile of dusty white feathers. He was lying quite still. Had I killed him? A sudden twitch and a rustling of feathers told me he was still alive. He shook his head in what I was certain was disbelief. I wondered what he would do next. I did not have long to wait. He stood, shook the dust from his feathers, and made another run for me. This time, I purposely jutted my violin case out in front of me. Defeated, Hannibal turned and walked away. I glanced around, expecting to see one warring angel at least. But no one was there. At least, no one I could see. I turned and strolled toward the house.

Hannibal never frightened or bothered me again.

Momma could hardly believe my story that afternoon as she examined my little black violin case, which bore a thick, deep scar down one side from Hannibal's spur. I had questions too. And while no one could explain to me how I had known to defend myself and how it all had happened, I thought I knew the answer. God had introduced Himself to me that day on the little dirt road. He had given me wisdom that my mind could not comprehend, but my spirit had understood completely. Late that fall, I was saved at the

Baptist church we went to every Sunday. Mr. Hancock came forward as I stood and prayed with me. Every Sunday after that, while the other kids would shuffle their feet, yawn, and make fans out of their Sunday school papers, I sat quietly and listened to Mr. Hancock talk about God. He would look over at me from time to time, our bond of understanding reinforced with a wink. And as I listened, all those stories seemed brand-new.

2

Mentor

I believe I can grow into a writer, I pray to God that I can be both … Then, I interview the sister of the Wright brothers who have invented the airplane. And Katherine tells of the heartbreaking years when they were ridiculed in their hometown of Dayton, Ohio. Simple bicycle mechanics, these "boys" over 30 spent their days messing with kites, gliders, an engine all smoke and noise. College professors had proved positively that men would never fly, yet Wilbur and Orville kept revising and retesting this "flying machine" that couldn't work. Their sister says to me simply, "And then, one day, it flew." Those words went back to the city room with me. They kept me from quitting then—or ever. Eventually came my first scoop, my first by-line, my first short story, my first book. … I've had disappointments. Stories rejected … But with each failure I've been able to chuckle a little, knowing that eventually, with patience and prayer, I could look back and say, "And then, one day, it flew!"[1]

She was well past eighty years old when I met her. A reporter for the Hearst newspapers, she had covered the Lindbergh baby kidnapping and the subsequent trial. She had interviewed the Prince of Wales following his abdication of the throne for "that Simpson woman," as she always called her. She had written about everything from sports to politics to Hollywood gossip. She had known Hoover (not the dam, not the president, but J. Edgar, himself), and she had lunched regularly with Clark Gable.

Me? Oh, I was quiet and shy and spent more time reading books than my parents thought was natural. In truth, I had been writing since grade school. I had spent much of the past few months writing letters to the editor of the local newspaper and had had them published several times. But my parents were mistaken about me. I was sure of it. I was not a journalist; I was simply a conundrum to them. I went to see this woman only to ease my momma's mind. She seemed so concerned about what would become of me. So much was her concern, and her seeming lack of confidence about my future, that I began to wonder myself.

One night, very late, I had gone to the kitchen for a glass of water. I could see the glow of a light shining beneath their door, and I knew they were still awake. I stopped to listen. They seemed deep in some sort of conversation. Momma was speaking.

"I don't know what is going to happen to her."

It wasn't long before my name was mentioned, and then there was absolute silence in the room. Then I heard Dad's voice.

"She'll be OK. Don't worry about her."

I tiptoed back to my bed and closed the door quietly, pondering the tiny bit of conversation I had overheard between my parents and sure it had been part of a much larger conversation about me. I knew very few things about life, but I knew beyond the shadow of a doubt that I had been born out of time. I did not like the 60s, miniskirts, go-go boots, or hippies. I did like the Beatles, and big band music. I was reserved and had few friends. I was barely sixteen years of age, and until I met this woman who was to be my mentor, I had never taken a risk, nor made many choices in my life.

This woman would pose a definite risk.

I walked up the rock path to her apartment, knocked, and entered. Her apartment was small, but comfortable. Stacks of books stood on every available space, and mounds of newspaper dotted the small table next to her armchair, where she was seated. She was small in stature, with wiry gray hair. She wore a pair of slacks and a neat blouse. Over this she was wearing an old vest that matched neither. She did not formally greet me, which I thought odd. I might not have been the person she had been expecting. Instead, she waved me in and seemed focused entirely on the television set that was pulled up to just feet away from her chair.

"Do you read?"

Those were her first words to me. I watched as she ran slender fingers through her thick gray hair like a comb. She did not look up at me but continued to stare at the television screen in her small sitting room. I said yes, but I was not sure that she had heard my response. My eyes left her and cut to the television screen. Merv Griffin was on, and so was my new mentor. There she was, sitting in the chair next to his desk. She was speaking about Richard Nixon. Apparently, Nixon had delivered groceries to her when he was a young boy.

"Good!" she said, causing me to jump, and I averted my eyes from the TV screen. She didn't seem to notice, anyway. "You must read."

She turned and cast about the table beside her chair. The pile of papers perched on it teetered and then spilled to the floor. She didn't seem to have minded much, because she didn't bother to retrieve them, nor ask me to pick them up. Out of the jumbled mess that was left on the table, she produced a pristine sheet of white paper and pen and handed them to me. My mouth fell open. How had she found anything in that mess? She then began to dictate to me a list of what would become a life list of authors I was to read as soon as possible: Thurber, Fitzgerald, Maugham, Salinger, Cather, Plath. I folded the paper and stuck it in my jacket pocket.

"Do you write?"

A commercial was on, and she managed to glance up at me properly for the first time. Before I could answer her, another question was fired at me.

"Do you like baseball?"

I said yes. I had been pondering the first question she had fired at me, and it had dovetailed with the second one. Yes—I enjoyed writing, and no, I did not like sports at all.

"What do you write?"

I told her I kept a journal. She told me that was good. Then she did the most amazing thing: she asked me to write a short story and bring it to our next meeting, and she would read it. Perh0aps, she added, she would enlist the expertise of an editor friend of hers to read it and provide me with a critique. My heart began to race. It was all happening so fast.

"Are you going to college?" I nodded, and she continued questioning me for over a half an hour. Her eyes, however, scarcely left the television set. Her questions remained short, to the point.

Our first meeting had left me both unsettled and excited. As I drove home, thoughts about myself, my life, my future whizzed about in my head. No sooner would I begin to concentrate on one than another would shove it aside, demanding to be noticed. And even though I answered her questions quickly and with confidence, I knew that my future lay around me unformed and shrouded in a mist. She did not seem to be the type to allow vagaries in her presence. I needed to know how I felt about myself, my writing, my goals.

When I arrived home, I went to my bedroom, closed the door softly behind me, and avoided contact with Momma. I dug through the bookcase on my desk and looked up the definition of a mentor. I didn't want to know the definition of the word, because I already knew it. I was looking for a way to disqualify this woman from being my mentor. She made me uncomfortable somehow. But neither Webster nor I could find a way to disallow her. I had to be honest: I was simply not from the world my mentor was from. My hardworking family would never have frequented the same restaurants as she did. My people were poor Okies who had come to California near the time of the dust bowl. They made quilts, culled potatoes, and worked in the fields pulling cotton or picking onions and oranges. They had rubbed elbows with lard to soften them after a hard day's work. This woman had rubbed elbows with Bebe Daniels, Garbo, and Chaplin. We did not seem to be from the same world. Yet she both frightened and fascinated me. I felt I could not relate to her in any way whatsoever, but she seemed to want to engage me, to help me. What would I decide? I sighed audibly and closed the dictionary, coming to a verdict. I chose her as my mentor, though I could not have told you why.

Her questions and criticisms of my hastily scrawled journal entries, which I would bring to her room each week, were precise and impersonal. There were endless questions regarding my use of tense, motivation of characters, plotlines, continuity. I watched as she drew line after line and tiny arrows across the pages of my notebook in bright pink ink. I had never known anyone to edit a journal. It made no sense. And always—always analogies between baseball and writing would come up.

"Like Tinker to Evers to Chance," she told me as she was going through a dissection of one of my journal entries.

Tinker, Evers, Chance—I did not know those writers. Discouraged, I reached into my handbag and pulled out my already dogeared list of authors that I had started at our first meeting. I jotted down three new names and then crossed them off later when I realized they were baseball players, not writers. I was beginning to like baseball even less, if that were possible.

Weeks passed before she would speak to me of things other than the mechanics of writing. She would spend much time recounting to me the situations she had found herself in as Hearst's first female reporter. It was a job she had taken when she was only nineteen years of age. Her stories fascinated me, and I sat and listened as this living, breathing history lesson spoke of presidents, politics, Hollywood stars she had known, and murder trials she had sat in on as a very young girl. Her father had been a famous lawyer in Los Angeles. She had experienced great losses as well. Her son had been a pilot, killed during World War 2. Her features seemed to soften a bit as she spoke of it.

"What did you do when you received the news?" I whispered. I had never known the death of a loved one up to that point in my life. I was horrified. I watched her fidget with the cap of the bright pink pen.

"When I got to the end of my rope," she said, her quiet tone matching my own, "I made a knot and held on."

She looked up and into my face. Her eyes were damp with tears. "Life brings changes."

Something in the room changed that day, though I could not tell you what it was. The way she related to me altered. Up until that point, she had demanded information from me. Now she was giving information about herself. I felt as if we were finally becoming acquainted.

We met whenever we could, usually weekly between classes. I was still in high school. I had penned a short story, and she sent it on to an editor she knew, Margaret Cousins, at *Ladies' Home Journal*. Cousins was going to read it and evaluate it. We looked at her reply in a note she had penned, telling my mentor that my writing "seems promising enough." I was elated, of course. It was a first effort, and we covered the basics of her recommendations as far as my style was concerned. But there were times when we would not work at all, but discuss some political issue of the day. Or she would talk and I would just sit, listening to her stories. She had many. We discovered many things we had in common: we had both been young when we had started to pursue our writing careers, and both had lived for a time in a single-parent home. At times, I would see her looking at me as if she were viewing herself at my age. I didn't mind so much.

That summer seemed to evaporate away, and soon another summer had replaced it. When I had met her, I was beginning my senior year of high school. Now I was in college, a journalism major. I was thinking of how quickly time had passed since our first meeting when I found myself drawn back into the conversation she was attempting to have with me. I caught only her last few words.

"And he is willing to give you a chance covering sports at his newspaper."

It had been those words that had brought me so forcefully out of my daydreams. She had taken the liberty of arranging an interview with someone: an editor of a large newspaper who thought I would be very interested in reporting sports news. I told her that was something I was not interested in. It took a very long time for her to respond.

"Well, why not?" It was the first time I had seen my mentor dumbfounded. She ran her fingers nervously and predictably through her hair, much as she did when she did not understand something that I had given her to read. Her hands returned to the armrests of the chair, and she leaned forward and looked directly into my eyes.

"Are you telling me you do not want to be a newspaper reporter?" she finally managed.

Another change had come in our relationship. My mentor came to understand and accept my refusal. My mentor and I parted company eventually. Our parting was not an awkward one. Her most recent book had been published, and the usual book signings, interviews, conferences, and television appearances would follow in rapid cadence. All these things would make our meetings more infrequent. My school schedule would conflict with our meetings as well. We parted as friends and kept in touch for a time. I heard a few years later that she had moved into the home of her daughter, who was also a writer.

My own career path changed as well. I had become a nurse, but always continued to write. I had several articles published. Soon, however, the largest outlet for my writing skills would be in patients' charts. Life, as my mentor had put it all those years ago, had brought changes to both of us.

When I found my mentor again, it was well over ten years later. Now in her mid-nineties, she was in a nursing home in the town where her daughter lived. I found my way to a small dayroom that held several chairs, a sofa, and a television set. A group of people sat silently in the room. Most had their eyes closed and seemed to be napping. Except for one. I spotted her at once; wispy white tendrils of hair peeked out from under a Chicago Cubs baseball cap. I would have known her anywhere. I went to her side and introduced myself. She looked up at me; her eyes met mine briefly but curiously. Then she smiled.

"Are you still writing?" she asked.

That short, direct question transported me. It was as if no time had passed since I had last walked through the door of her small apartment those long years ago. I told her I did, and that I had been published. Drawing a small chair to sit near her for a while, I felt my heart overflow with gratitude for this wise and eccentric lady.

There are individuals who come our way for a purpose. I had known God to use pillars of fire, plagues, and bushes that caught fire to gain the attention of His people. He did this to guide and protect them and show them the path before them. My mentor had given me the ability to find my own voice and a direction for my life. I knew God had sent this mentor to me. Her name was Adela Rogers St. Johns.

I began to thank her for all those things, and more. I continued to babble on for a few moments; then I noticed a strange, stern look creep over her face. I felt a chill of recognition. I had seen that face before. It was the same look she had given me when I told her I had no intentions of being a newspaper reporter. She absently pulled at the bill of her baseball cap and raised a finger, bidding me come closer.

"Would you move aside, please?" she asked quietly, but firmly. "You're blocking the TV." I looked over at the television, smiled, and slid the chair over to one side. Her hand reached out and held mine as she continued to watch. You see, it was baseball, after all, and it was the bottom of the ninth.

3

Clutter

Grandma had fallen during the past winter. She had gotten up in the middle of the night for a glass of water and had fallen somewhere near the kitchen. For the past two months, she had been in a nursing center, undergoing rehabilitation. Grandpa had gone along, unwilling to be parted from her. At the end of her therapy, Grandpa began to develop a bit of debility, and it was recommended that he remain in the nursing center for some therapy. Grandma, of course, unwilling to be parted from him, agreed that they would both spend the winter at the nursing center. Momma and I arranged things and then began the process of closing their home and making it secure for the long, cold winter ahead. We had seen to the furnace and made sure all doors and storm windows were secured.

We made our way through the bathroom and kitchen and arrived on the back porch, which was the site of Grandma's accident earlier that fall. I stood there looking for a moment, thinking of how best we could winterize a back porch of a home built in the 1940s and looking for obstacles like the one Grandma had tripped over, causing her fall. I inspected the floor and discovered an old cotton rug placed between the kitchen and porch, possibly the cause of her accident that fall. It slid easily with my foot, and I pushed it into a corner; then I flung the storage cupboards open wide above the washer and dryer. I was looking for a nonskid rug to replace the slippery cotton one. What greeted me was the sight of stacks of yellow butter tubs. Thousands of them.

"Hey," I called to Momma, who was in the kitchen. "What should we do with these?"

As if protesting the possibility of their removal, they tumbled in all directions. Gratefully, they weighed little. Momma, hearing the clatter, poked her head around the doorway to the porch.

"Oh wow, do those things have lids?" Momma said excitedly, her eyes bright as she surveyed the sea of yellow oleo tubs. I scowled.

We both understood why Grandma had kept them. Of course we did. We were both recalling little stacks of things around our own homes, hidden in the recesses of lonely closets, under sinks, behind stacks of bath towels. Oh yes, we understood completely!

We moved stealthily into the basement, where a single, aged lightbulb hung from a black cloth cord in the exact center of the room, where anyone walking about would bang his or her head on it. *Poor planning,* I thought as it popped me on the side of my head and sent wisps of spiderweb and dust flying in all directions.

"Oh, here they are!" Momma had gone around me to a rickety shelf and pulled down an open box filled with grimy, web-laced discs. Momma had found the lids to the butter tubs. I made a note to check her luggage before she left to return to California.

The things we keep!

I returned to the house after the first big snow, bringing in a few trash bags, and headed for the back porch. I tossed the slippery cotton rug in the trash bin and replaced it with a new, latex-backed one. The house was warm. We had left the electric on, and the gas floor furnace was working. The dry, dusty smell of the floor furnace hit me as I entered the living room. I grabbed a dry rag and cleaned the top of the floor register. I sprayed another rag with dusting spray and wiped down furniture and tables. I could not locate a vacuum cleaner. With the house smelling like a lemon grove, I continued my quest.

With a complete lack of sentimentality, I returned to the back porch and piled the old yellow butter tubs in the plastic trash bin, reminding myself to get the lids as well, in case Momma returned that spring to claim them. I loaded a second filled black trash bag into the trunk of our car and walked cautiously up the snowy walkway to the house. Truthfully, I had been blaming myself for Grandma's fall. Of course, I had had nothing to do with it; it had been an accident. I wondered if I could have taken time to have prevented it. Was I cleaning Grandma's house as some sort of penance? The clutter of guilt weighed on my mind and my heart.

I recalled, years earlier, having God forgive me of a past failure in my life. Yet the simple remembrance of it had stuck to me, as if by static cling. God had graciously walked me through that time. My sin had not disqualified me from serving Him but had built total reliance upon Him. I was grateful for the Holy Spirit's reminder of this. I could not have helped what had happened to Grandma, but I could make her a clean and safe place for her and Grandpa to come home to. I returned to the house, free of the heaviness I had felt.

I passed the old breakfront cabinet near the dining table, dragging the empty trash bin behind me. A search through the first drawer told me I had discovered Grandma's junk drawer. It was clogged with old bits of wire, several old hearing aids, various small tools and desk items. In short, things that had nowhere else to go had gone there to hide, out of sight and hopefully out of mind.

I had things like that.

I began tossing unnecessary things like the broken bits of wire, old bottle caps, and other items into the trash bin. That drawer was so busy it was impossible to find anything, even if the things it held had been useful. Busy. I scraped handfuls into the plastic trash bin, thinking to myself that I could have come here to help Grandma long before this. But I had been ... busy. In addition to being a farm wife, with a job and tending to the home and our young daughter, Sarah, I had projects at church. I say *projects* because that is a term that applies to many words. There were committees, meetings of all sorts, ministries without actual names. Busyness can become a ministry. It is sly that way. It begins to speak to us of more once we get entangled in things—more meetings, more teaching tapes, more conferences, more Bible studies. There were stacks of books in my office, and piles of magazines, and copies of articles that people had given me, thinking I would be interested in them. They literally made a paperscape along one wall of my desk. But I had noticed that the cascade of things going on around me, though godly, had left me with very little downtime to absorb what I had learned before going on to the next thing. Not to mention my own personal time of reflection, which seemed, like those coils of wire and mismatched bolts in Grandma's junk drawer, to have gone somewhere to hide until the busyness of it all was over.

Well, as it happened, it was Sunday morning. And here I was, elbow deep in a junk drawer. Did I feel guilty, like I had backslid? Nope. Pray for me if you think that is wrong, but I had long since abandoned the gravitational pull of busyness in my own life. I believe this experience with Grandma brought my attention to it. If we are not learning and growing closer to God, we are wasting our time with programs and books and speakers. Ministry is not a contest to see who can be busiest, or who is slacking. And the spiritual clutter of busyness could very easily restrict or obscure paths God has for us. I smiled and picked up the trash bin, which was a lot heavier. God understood my absence this morning. After all, I was on a mission trip to Grandma's infamous linen closet.

I was not surprised when I opened it to see that nothing had changed since the last time Grandma had opened it in my presence a year earlier. She had always instructed me that this was to be done carefully. She opened the slender door just a crack at first and then slowly let the door fall open. With that, an old quilt, along with several other items, fell out. The quilt flopped out, covering her head, and she giggled. Then I saw her look down. She had spied something on the floor.

"Oh!" she exclaimed as she pulled the quilt off her head and tossed it to me to fold. It seemed, however, that she had forgotten what she had initially been looking for and had settled on some long-lost item that had toppled out onto the floor at her feet. It would take the two of us to close the door to the closet safely again.

I looked the closet over for a moment. All it needed was to be organized a bit, I reasoned, and began placing blankets in a neat stack. Next, I set the tablecloths into a pile, and then doilies. I lifted shelf after shelf of items away until the piles were all laid neatly out on top of the dining table. As I began to refold the items and ready them to go back into the linen closet, I wondered what they might be thinking at church. I could hear them grilling Galen about my whereabouts, and the plans they would be making without me. The more I thought, the more frustrated I became. Those thoughts seemed to gain a life of their own as I continued to ponder them. I found myself angry at some of the women, especially those who seemed to have a finger on the pulse of every mission, every new book, every seminar, every women's meeting. I felt judged as I stood there making little towers out of Grandma's linens and was nearly ensnared by my own thoughts. *Peace,* I thought. Peace wasn't easy to maintain at times. I was amazed at how a single, unguarded thought had become a false reality and attacked my mind. For all I knew, no one had noticed my absence at all.

Often in our spiritual walk, guilt, lack of control over our thoughts, grief, self-doubt, and feelings of discouragement come to us. We may compare ourselves to others in ministry, our performance coming up short in our own eyes. There have been times when I have felt stuck. The dreams are not being realized quickly enough, and a weariness settles over me from the waiting. That is when we lean very close to Him. He has the cure for all our anxieties:

> Humble yourselves, therefore, under God's mighty hand, that he may lift you up in due time. Cast all your anxiety on him because he cares for you. (1 Peter 5:6–7 NIV)

I returned to the back porch. Access to the old basement was in the floor at one side of the porch. I did not like going down there.

Grandma never ventured much down their either, as she could not pull the trap door up enough to latch it to the heavy hook on the wall. Grandpa had always been assigned that chore. The basement, which ran all the way under the house, was cool, and the walls were thick fieldstone. The steps were heavy wood and quite sturdy, considering the entire scene felt as if I were entering an abyss of darkness. My eyes never seemed to adjust to the light, or lack of, down in the basement, and I moved my arms around in the darkness, flailing about for the light pull. This place seemed to catch all the things in the house that had lost their usefulness. It smelled damp and dusty, both at the same time. At once, I discovered where Grandma's vacuum cleaner had been put. I soon realized that it no longer worked; nor did the three others that sat neatly next to it against the cool stone wall. I wondered why we all have that tendency to cling to useless things. I grabbed the old box filled with butter tub lids and tossed them up the stairs and onto the porch floor. *One less thing,* I thought. Buckets, and a few old mops that were broken and beyond usefulness, were brought upstairs and placed in the trash bin. I had brought my own vacuum cleaner, and I spent the remainder of the morning cleaning the carpets and rugs in each room. At last, the house was clean.

As I made my last trip out of the house, toting my bucket, mop, and vacuum cleaner, things felt different to me. I felt grateful for the time at Grandma's house, cleaning and decluttering it. Taking out the garbage that day was like taking out the garbage in my own heart and leaving the lessons learned in place. As I arrived home, a fresh mission field beckoned me: my back porch. Filled with the victories that were mine following my previous mission trip, I opened the small utility closet to place the vacuum cleaner back in its place and felt the handle of my mop bang me solidly on top of my head. I laughed, rubbed my head, and continued the work. By the end of the night, I had a knot on my head—and a clean porch.

That night, I went into my office and cleaned off my desk. There, next to my computer, I placed a single yellow butter tub, which I had filled with paperclips. A reminder to abide, uncluttered.

4

The Search

God never opens doors that have been closed. He opens other doors, but He reminds us that there are doors which have been shut, doors which we have shut, doors which need never have been shut, imaginations which need never have been sullied. Never be afraid when God brings back the past. Let memory have its way. It is a minister of God with its rebuke and chastisement and sorrow. God will turn the "might have been" into a wonderful culture for the future.[1]

I could tell this story like a fairytale—though it did not start out that way. It is the story of a father who had a daughter who loved him beyond measure. One day the father gathered all his belongings in an old bag and journeyed far, far away—away from the daughter who loved him, and who did not understand what had happened to make him go away. Days turned into weeks, weeks to months, and months to years. Then, one day, she saw her father again. Something had changed. She came to realize that she did not know this man— her father. She wondered about him, and had to decide: Did she want to know him, or was he to forever remain a stranger? And she wondered why she could not remember him.

There is something about the start to a story, like a fairytale; something that draws us in, makes us want to discover more. Like an unmarked box. It is a curiosity, and you want to look inside. Often it is simply marked "storage," which gives no clue to its contents. It is nearly always underfoot, taking up space. When I find myself unpacking such boxes, I do so with great care. I have put things away before and forgotten where I have put them, thinking them lost forever. Things like memories of growing up with my father. *Surely, I must have a few,* I would reason within myself. Yet they simply were not there. Somehow, I had put them away in a place where I could no longer reach them. I believe that we all have those secret corners. Unnamed, unmarked, but calling out to us, determined to be recognized. I am amazed when something is brought forth and laid bare before me, bearing the unmistakable postmark of heaven upon it. God uses many ways to convey His purpose in our lives: circumstance, situations, locations, and that uneasy feeling inside our spirits. He doesn't use them to betray us, but to free us. Even using our senses, like a scent.

The smell of a familiar, nameless flower drifted through the air. Borne on the thick tropical air, the scent stirred some vague memories within me as we walked the short connecting corridor from the airplane to the terminal building at Honolulu International Airport. We had just completed the long flight on our way to a well-deserved family vacation. It occurred to me that the very hallway I was walking in had not even existed all those years ago. The year had been 1961. In fact, the plane would land on the landing tarmac, and those arriving would disembark and walk on the tarmac to the terminal. But it wasn't the location and the changes that had me thinking. Memories of a little girl in paradise those many years ago were not comfortable to me. Each time I had thought of our vacation, it evoked a jumble of emotions.

I looked around us as we got into the taxi that shuttled us to our hotel for our eight-day stay. Oahu had changed. I had changed, too, returning to it with a husband and two-year-old daughter, Sarah. Exhausted from the trip, Sarah crumpled into a small, sweet heap on one of the beds in our hotel room. My husband, Galen, sat out on the lanai, drinking in the warm tropical evening and the din of traffic below our fourth-floor room. I had been thinking back to a time of prayer I had had shortly before our trip. In those days, I prayed grandiose prayers. I asked for things I was in no way able to handle if I were to get them. It was, of course, no wonder that many of them had gone unanswered, or seemed to. But not this one. I wondered precisely why I had been so adamant about returning here, when I didn't want to be there at all. It was a dream vacation for our family, and I was not ungrateful for it. God had seemed to speak an answer almost immediately, and His answer made me bristle. He had something to show me there.

I had lived on the island with my parents and two younger sisters. After our return to the mainland some three years later, we eventually settled in the Central Coast area of California, in a small farming community near the ocean. My life would be drastically and forever changed when my parents divorced quite suddenly. As I got a bit older, I realized that this island had been the last place I had recalled feeling as if I had a home, that I was safe, that I had a family. Memories flooded in as I sat there watching Sarah sleep soundly. One was of the day my father left, and the other was sitting in a long, hardwood pew filled with aunts and uncles and cousins. It was my grandfather's funeral. At that time, I had not seen my father in over eight years. Now, here we all were, drawn together for a short time in our grief. My grief, however, seemed doubled somehow. Not only had I lost my grandpa, but the disconnection between my father and me seemed unresolvable. I glanced down the row and saw my father sitting quietly, tears staining his face. He seemed so broken-hearted. I knew how he felt. I had lost my father, too.

These were the thoughts that had intruded upon me now, here. They had followed me to this beautiful place where I shouldn't have a care in the world except to watch a sunrise, play in the sand with my husband and young daughter, and then watch the sunset over the glorious Pacific Ocean in paradise. I was not certain what God was trying to show me. What was the point of dredging up things all over again? The simple truth was, I did not have any memories of my father when he had lived with us. The standard explanation from Momma had been that he had been away working most of the time. But I had always clung stubbornly to the idea that I must have had memories somewhere. They were just hidden away somewhere, waiting for me to find them. I would attempt at times to shake my mind by looking at stacks of old black-and-white photos from my childhood. My father would be there, standing right next to me, holding me, and I was of an age where I should have recalled the event, but I didn't. Myself, sitting on a tractor beside my father. Nothing. So, I set my search aside. Perhaps the little girl sitting next to my father had been someone else, and not me at all.

We spent our first full day searching for the perfect beach. We did not have to go far. I could not wait to fill my bag with pencils, a good book, and my journal and spend each moment documenting our vacation. But there were no notes taken, no shining moments of creativity to jot into my journey. Instead, my mind went strangely ide, not sticking at all to the plan I had so cleverly devised before we left. I sat and watched the waves curl rhythmically against the shoreline that entire day.

"Momma!"

Our daughter, Sarah, brought me back from my long reflections. I stared down the long expanse of uninterrupted white sand and watched her run toward me. She plopped herself down on the mat beside me, scattering sand all over me. She opened her tiny hand, revealing to me her treasures. She had a broken clam shell, a knob of well-worn coral, and a tangle of fishing line. I smiled at them. She watched the shore with me for a while, and then she spied her father swimming just offshore in the surf. She ran toward him, and he lifted her up onto his shoulder in one effortless motion. And in that moment of observation, a memory came. I saw another little girl in my mind's eye, her slim, tanned arms reaching up for her father. She scampered between the breakers, waiting for him. At just the right moment, he lifted her up into his arms above the crashing waves. They were laughing and smiling. You could tell he loved her very much. I felt enveloped in the experience. And I realized that memory had been real. The little girl had been me. Where had this memory come from? I certainly hadn't asked for it or conjured it up. But there it was.

By midweek, I had emptied my bag of all but a single notebook and pencil and added Sarah's sand pail. Sand soon invaded the spaces between the pages of the empty notebook, and it, too, was soon left behind in the hotel room. My thoughts, like my beach bag, had been pared down to only the essentials as we traveled to the northernmost part of the island. The beaches here were rocky, and the shoreline dropped quickly away into the sea in places. We made ourselves a place to sit near some large, ocean-washed rocks a safe distance from the precarious tide and shoreline. Sarah sat contentedly, talking to the rocks, and made a game of carrying pail after pail of them from one corner of the mat and dumping them in a pile at the opposite end.

Now, I knew from years of experiences as a beachcomber that the best shells and other treasures could be found just beneath these mounds of water-worn stones, often just out of sight. Bits of sea glass soon began to emerge: tabs of milky blue, green, and white. Sarah delighted in her newfound job of carrying away the stones as I searched. I looked up and around me for a time, my back hurting from bending and searching for shells, and realized that I had been at that beach before. I had been there on a picnic with my family. Remembrances of that picnic were spotty; there was another family with us, and a baby, and the waves were very large. We had been happy there.

"Keep?" Sarah asked. She had found a perfect cowrie shell about an inch long.

I nodded. "Keep."

Hanauma Bay had been a place I had visited many times as a child. Momma would brave the steep volcanic rock steps down to the beach with us, and I honestly didn't see how she had done it as we walked with Sarah, who seemed to be going faster than her legs were able to manage. Finally, we corralled her between us and walked slowly together. The steps were steep switchbacks, sloping down and opening to a pristine white beach and clear blue water, perfect for snorkeling. We found a place to make our beach nest for the afternoon and slathered ourselves with sunscreen. I reached into my nearly vacant denim beach bag and pulled out a face mask I had bought at a vendor in Honolulu when we arrived on the island. It was Sarah's size exactly. Her dad slipped the mask around her head and then told her to dunk her head just into the water.

At first, she was a bit apprehensive. But soon she nearly had her entire head under the water, rising only for a bit of air. At last, she rose and stayed above water long enough to shout, "Fish!" A group of delicate angelfish had fluttered toward her, followed by a clownfish. They swarmed the front of her mask, making her jump back, giggle, and then force her head back down into the water, hoping for another encounter. She pulled the mask off after a time, seeming to lose interest in it when she saw the sea glass and shells popping out of the sand near our mat. But that night, she hopped in the tub with the mask, and it lay safely next to her pillow as she slept.

So many memories had been hidden from me, like the sea glass treasures and shells that filled a small jar sitting next to me, lying just out of sight, just below the covering of beach stones. As I began the task of packing to go home early the following morning, I found myself almost unwilling to go. I was bringing much more back than I had arrived with. Memories had been restored to me, and new ones had been made.

The following morning, we waited outside the hotel for our taxi. A light, misty rain began to fall during a beautiful sunrise. Tiny droplets of water hung in the air, saturated with light, and appeared as glittering diamonds all around us. Sarah had seen it too. She raised her little hands up, trying to catch them. She looked at me, disappointed, when she held her hands open and they were gone. I remembered the rain that looked like diamonds from my childhood. We would run out onto the lawn when it would rain and try to gather the gems in our hands, only to be as disappointed as Sarah had been when we could not retrieve any of them. This had been a magical place to a young girl who had lived in paradise so long ago.

The taxi arrived, and I reached for my old denim beach bag. It was fat with the things we had gathered on our trip. I thought of my heart as that beaten-up old bag, filled to overflowing with both needful and unnecessary items, like it had been on the beach during the first few days of our trip. Then, slowly, it had been emptied to only the essentials—the necessary things. Things that would have distracted me on this trip had disappeared, and what remained was the discovery of memories I had never known I had. No—He had not changed my past, but He had forever altered the way I would perceive it.

Sarah squirmed as the plane lifted into the sky, and we looked purposefully out the window; we hoped to catch a last glimpse of the island before the clouds obscured our view. And then, it was gone. We settled back in our seats for the long flight back to the mainland. Sarah reached into her pocket and pulled out a thick chunk of milky blue sea glass. One of her treasures. I thought of the changes that little bit of glass had gone through, the transformation it had made. It had not received its patina overnight. It took months, perhaps years, of sitting patiently on that sea floor, whipped by the continual tides and ground by the sand, until it was discovered by us. Something that had begun as something broken, discarded, had been rediscovered and transformed. I had placed my denim bag beneath the seat in front of me once we had boarded the plane. My eyes fell on the dog-eared travel brochure someone had thrust into my hand at the airport when we had arrived.

"Oahu: The Gathering Place," it read.

Aptly named, I thought. To my joy, the memories that I had begun gathering continued to return to me long after our vacation ended. They were not complete; just bits and pieces of thoughts, and feelings, and smells. Memories. These would be my greatest treasures and would open doors beyond anything I could have imagined with my father.

After that trip, we began to establish a relationship with my father. We had gone to see him several times at his home in California. Once when Sarah was a toddler, and once when she was nearly six. On that visit, we walked in a little park near the sea. The rides that had been there for the tourists were closing. I watched as my father slipped a bill into the hand of a young man, who turned the carousel lights back on. A few minutes later, Sarah was the sole occupant of the carousel for at least fifteen minutes. She beamed at us as she passed us and waved at her grandpa each time she rounded the corner where we stood.

Through the years, my father also visited us at our home. He loved the Midwest, with its changing seasons. His visits nearly always brought up old memories for him of living with his mother and sisters in Tulsa. We enjoyed taking him to familiar places he had known as a boy. The last time I was to see my father, he was recuperating from a bout of pneumonia and was recovering in an assisted living facility in Henderson, Nevada. I was able to spend time with him, watching how he interacted with the other residents, going to daily exercise class, and having a fresh audience for all his old jokes. Dad was always cheerful every time we visited him. As we were leaving to return home, I visited him one last time. He took my hand and demanded my full attention.

"I love you," he said.

Somewhere inside me, the little girl who had searched for so many years for her memories of her father rejoiced at his words. It was the best thing that a little girl could ever hear from her father.

Within a month of our visit, he died, at the age of ninety.

5

The Swimsuit

Give me all of you!!! I don't want so much of your time, so much of your talents and money, and so much of your work. I want YOU!!! ALL OF YOU!! I have not come to torment or frustrate the natural man or woman, but to KILL IT! No half measures will do. I don't want to only prune a branch here and a branch there; rather I want the whole tree out! Hand it over to me, the whole outfit, all of your desires, all of your wants and wishes and dreams. Turn them ALL over to me, give yourself to me and I will make of you a new self—in my image. Give me yourself and in exchange I will give you Myself. My will, shall become your will. My heart, shall become your heart.[1]

I was a hopeless wallflower in school. Like most high-schoolers, I realized early on that school was heavy on the law and light on grace. And what was the law? Popularity, being smart, belonging to the right clique, being a cheerleader or being a member of the pep squad. I always struggled with feeling as if I did not fit in. In any social situation, I found myself melting into the background. My heart, however, wanted desperately to be a part of something. When

I received news of a ten-year high school reunion, I decided at once not to go. Now I sat at a table filled with what was left of the other wallflowers I had graduated with. An announcement came from the front table: the winner of the person who had travelled the furthest to attend the reunion was … me. A second announcement soon followed the first: the award for the best memory of high school. Feeling clever, I had scribbled my remembrance out several months earlier. It had not been a memory of a pretty prom dress, nor an academic achievement. It had been a story I had written called "The Swimsuit," about the suits the girls had to wear in our PE class in our senior year. I mailed it to the reunion committee. Somehow, it had made the cut, and had given me a second honor that night: the best memory of high school belonged to me, as well.

The swimsuits we girls wore during PE were curious articles of clothing. Wide, boxy, basically shapeless, they were made of some sort of thick tee-shirt material that, when wet, sagged and bagged dreadfully. All were faded royal blue. Before each of us went out, we all stood in line, some having their friends pin the back straps together with a huge, blunted safety pin to keep the suits on us while we were in the water. We dipped under a quick shower once we were clad in our suits and had pinned ourselves. We then made our way up the ramp to the pool area just outside the locker room and make our way to the shallow end of the pool.

It was the usual horrible day for me in the locker room. I dreaded this time of day more than chemistry class. The usual group of girls would stare at me, point at me, comment on my lack of features. Loudly. I turned my back on them, embarrassed. My face felt hot, and I would always pretend I had not heard their comments. I stripped and slipped into the too-big suit and began the struggle of pinning myself up in the back. I had two pins. I had found one in an empty locker near mine, held onto it, and used it.

All of us made our way up the ramp. The girls talked and giggled amongst themselves, some gathered into small knots while they rechecked to make sure their pins were secure on their suits. We entered the pool area. Some girls wandered around the perimeter and entered at the shallower end, taking the steps into the cool water. Others dove in. I simply got in as quickly as I could to avoid being seen by the line of boys who were on their way to the baseball diamond. The water always felt lovely. On that day, I lingered at the deep end. I floated on my back. I sank slowly beneath the water and did a double summersault. I rose quickly from the bottom of the pool, and as I reached the surface, I realized that all the girls had already gathered at the meeting place. The teacher had everyone's attention, and I was not there. I flailed about for a moment as I thought of the fastest way to reach them. Then a sudden, horrifying realization came to me. I reached behind me to feel for my pins on the back of my suit. They were not there. Neither was my swimsuit.

I slid beneath the water again as quietly as I could. My eyes stung from the over-chlorinated water, but soon I saw a lone, misshapen blue object wafting under me at the nine-foot level under the water. It looked somewhat like a billowy manta ray with two very large safety pins attached to it—just floating there. My suit! I rose to the surface. The teacher was still speaking, giving directions. I slid under again. I dove deep under the water, retrieved the suit, and slipped back into it. Somehow—I don't know how—I had managed to swim right out of my suit without being seen and was very much hoping it would stay that way. The pins were tricky, but I got it done. I resurfaced slowly, deliberately. A whistle blew. The teacher had seen me at last and waved me over impatiently. I swam toward the group with deep, broad strokes. I had done it! I did not know how it had happened—to lose my swimsuit, then to find it, and then to put it back on without anyone knowing I had done it. But I had. No one knew. No one.

Though it was not read aloud, applause and laughter followed a brief synopsis of the article. After a time, I made my way to the restroom. The event was held at the school, and I found myself in the very locker room I had been in years earlier. It wasn't long before several ladies wandered in. I recognized one of them at once. It was one of the girls who had ridiculed me in PE class, in that very room. She walked past me as if she hadn't seen me, tugging at her dress. She soon noticed me in the reflection in the mirror.

"You look nice," she announced as she pulled again on her evening dress. It was pretty, but clearly ill-fitting somehow. She had always been very well endowed, and though I had not been a good student in science, I recognized the effect of gravity and age on the human body.

"Thanks," I replied, trying to smile, and trying not to stare at her.

She pointed to her reflection. "This is a what-not-to-wear-to-a-reunion dress." She gave the dress one final tug. "Ugh! I thought it would still fit me," she said. She walked toward the door to return to the noisy gymnasium and then stopped.

"I liked your story, by the way." She smiled, and as she passed, she gave me a quick hug and smile.

I stared for a moment in the ancient mirror over the sink and wondered at the possibility that it might be original equipment from when I had once graced that room a decade earlier. I was still a wallflower, but a better version somehow. I felt I had grown up, become less afraid, less worried, less concerned with what anyone thought. I knew something else: I knew that God had been there that day at the pool. He had known the depth of my shyness and embarrassment, as well as my sadness at being teased. He also knew that it would be something that would resolve itself, eventually. I had always imagined it was He who had held up that swimsuit just above the bottom of the pool that day, waiting for me to glimpse it and retrieve it. I thought again of the swimsuit, and I had to smile. I wished I could have kept one. I was sure they were all long gone. After all, they had been old, faded, and stretched out when we'd used them years ago. I recalled the last great day of swimming class, as I placed one large safety pin into the scuffed brown box held by the teacher. The other one I had hidden in my binder, the reminder of a great victory.

That night, as I wandered away from the reunion, saying goodbye to classmates, I knew that I was no longer the same person who had once graced the halls of that locker room a decade earlier, and no one was more surprised at that than me. I was intensely aware of His presence and the work He had done in me. I was not sure where all my concerns, fears, sadness, and brokenheartedness had gone. But I felt certain I knew when they had released their firm grip on me: it was when I climbed out of the pool that day and walked back to the locker room. Somehow, some way, those feelings and criticisms, the incessant teasing and ridicule I had known, were gone. And they never returned. It is my belief (and I still believe it to this day) that they remained at the bottom of the pool that day, somewhere near the nine-foot marker.

I stopped at my car and reached into the pocket of my dress slacks, retrieving a single, very old, very large safety pin. I pulled it out and looked at it for a moment. Somehow, I had felt I had to bring it with me that night. I held it in my hand, recalling those who had fought great battles and been victorious. They would often bring back trophies or tokens as reminders: sabers, guns, flags, even treasures from their enemies.

I have an old safety pin.

6

The Message

The circumstances of a saint's life are ordained of God. In the life of a saint there is no such thing as chance. God by His providence brings you into circumstances that you cannot understand at all, but the Spirit of God understands. ... All your circumstances are in the hand of God, therefore never think it strange concerning the circumstances you are in.[1]

I have heard God speak to me. Not audibly, but in my heart, with a sure knowing. At times, it comes from the confirming and comforting words of others to me. I have known people who have heard the audible voice of God. I believe them. I believe God can use whatever He wants to get to people, to help, to heal, to bring closure or information about an open door of ministry to someone who is in desperate need. And, of course, to bring His message of salvation. I know this because I have experienced it myself many times. The first time it happened, however, I was not so sure of any of it, especially myself.

I breezed past the nursing station and down the shiny, white-tiled hall to room seventeen. I had walked those halls for several years as a charge nurse, but this evening was different. One of my patients, Hiram, was very ill. At eighty years of age, Hiram was worn down from recurring infections that had left him frail and fighting for his life. When morning came, the Veteran's Hospital van would arrive and take him on a long ride away from our small town. Perhaps take him from us forever. I stopped in the hall outside Hiram's room. I was thinking of his physical condition. Would he understand the reason for my visit? Then there was the other side, the real reason I had come to see him in the first place.

I had been at work that day. As I approached Hiram's room that morning, I heard these words: *Hiram does not know me.*

No, it wasn't in a booming voice. I was just walking by his room, and I knew it. What's more, these words were not new to me. I had dreamt of them earlier that week. Throughout the day, while working at the nursing station, feeding patients, or checking the halls, the voice would come. Always the same words. I felt bullied by the words I had heard and dreamt of that week. I would not know what to say to Hiram. Hiram was a stubborn and argumentative man. He was also very, very sick. I left work without talking to him.

The phone was ringing as I walked through our door. It was Phyllis, my Avon lady.

"I know you're off work now. I just hate to bother you."

"No, that's all right, Phyllis. What can I do for you?" In a small, vacant part of my brain I was busily making up an Avon order for her, as I assumed that was why she had called me. She had dropped a brochure on the desk earlier that week.

"It's just that I've been thinking about Hiram." I knew that Phyllis and Hiram had lived on farms in the southern part of the county, and their families had been lifelong friends. "Amy, I don't think he's saved. Do you think you could go talk to him this evening?"

I was stunned. Phyllis had no way of knowing—I had told no one about the words I had been sensing.

"Let me see if I can get our pastor over there tonight," I offered.

"No!" she said at once, and firmly. "I just know it has to be you. I know that sounds crazy."

No, it did not sound crazy. I knew she was right. I picked my purse and keys back up and drove the seven miles back to town. Within twenty minutes, I had arrived at the nursing home. Now—here I was standing at his door.

I knocked softly, and he did not respond. I gently edged the door open. The room was a simple one, mirroring all the others in the building. A twin bed, a small bedside table, and a dresser. Along one wall, a closet. Hiram lay in bed, facing the wall. The strong smell of urine permeated the room, and I knew he had been too weak to use the urinal properly. A puddle lay beside the bed; his bedcovers were soaked. He was so still that I wondered if I was too late to talk to him. I closed the door behind me. There had been too many events that week that had brought me to that room, at that moment, at that time. I had a message for him.

Hiram moaned and rolled over in his bed. He held out his arm to me, possibly thinking I was going to take his blood pressure again. It was then that I realized that I hadn't changed out of the uniform I had worn that day. I came closer. I doubted he would be able to converse with me. With great effort, he opened his eyes and asked me to raise him up in bed. I bunched his pillow behind his back and propped him up.

I want you to be my witness today.

I want you to tell him that I love him.

I pulled the chair close to his bed and sat, and we talked. His life had been a difficult one. He had struggled with bad health for many years.

"I'm tired of fighting it all, you know. All I think I want to do is go home," he muttered. "I just want to go home."

I knew what he meant. At least, I thought I did. I thought he was speaking of going back to the old farmhouse he'd lived in for years. Back to a comfortable place he had known and loved. But that was not what he meant.

"I just want to die. Can you all just let me die?" he said quietly.

Tell him.

I sat there and looked into the face of that old man. For several days, I had felt unable to deliver the message I knew God had been encouraging me to give Hiram. But there was an overwhelming sense of the Lord's presence in the room, and with it the knowledge that this was Hiram's time to hear this message and my time to give it. Whatever questions I had come in with, whatever inadequacies I had felt, whatever doubts I had seemed to melt away at that moment.

We talked for a very long time. I gave Hiram the message, and Hiram prayed a simple prayer of salvation with me. I sat with him afterward, and just before he fell asleep, he tried to explain what had happened inside him as he prayed that prayer with me that night.

"I don't know how to say this—it just felt like my old heart was like a lock all covered with rust, like old barb wire. Then that old lock just burst open." He managed a weak smile at this and patted my hand.

I returned home that night and phoned Phyllis. She cried. We both did.

Hiram left the following morning for the VA facility. Much to the amazement of his caregivers at the VA hospital, he made excellent progress and returned to our facility. His infection was gone, and he had even gained a little weight. A crowd of staff gathered in the hallway to welcome him back and settle him in his little room. The girls settled him in bed and left, and I filled his water pitcher.

When I got there to his room, a family friend, Madeline, stood there, her arms filled with freshly laundered overalls, Hiram's usual and favored wardrobe.

"You know, his sister has been praying for him for years," she said, staring down at Hiram. He had fallen asleep as soon as his head had hit his pillow. Madeline's eyes shifted to me. "She prayed someone would come his way and help him receive Jesus," she said quietly. "I believe God sent you."

During his stay at the hospital, Hiram's very elderly sister had called me during one of my shifts. With a quavering voice she thanked God, and then thanked me, and she thanked the doctors and nurses who had cared for him. I assured her that God had been faithful, and He had answered her prayers. She had been praying for him for over fifty years. I was amazed at this woman and in awe of God, who had not forgotten that one persistent prayer of a loving and godly sister.

Hiram soon settled back into his routine at the nursing home. He was still obstinate with some of the staff, but whenever he saw me in the hallway, he would always come and hug me and smile. He even began attending some of the services held at the home each Sunday.

I have often thought of what Madeline had said to me the day Hiram returned from the hospital: that God had sent me. What Madeline had said was true, but only in part. When I recalled everything that had transpired to bring Hiram's salvation to pass, I knew in my heart that I had not walked into his room alone. Three women had entered that room and sat at his bedside that night. First, there was a tenacious elderly sister, standing tall and clad in the mantle of a mighty prayer warrior; beside her, the Avon lady who had brought clarity and confirmation; last, there was the messenger, on her journey into the things of God, learning to listen and obey. Above all was the tangible, gracious presence of God, who had been merciful not only to the unbeliever, but to the timid messenger as well.

I was grateful that night for both.

7

The Bullfrog and the Tractor

We can all see God in exceptional things, but it requires the culture of spiritual discipline to see God in every detail. Never allow that the haphazard is anything less than God's appointed order, and be ready to discover the Divine designs anywhere.[1]

Galen had been accustomed to me calling out to him when I was sorting family photos. There were evenings when he would simply sit at the table, bringing his reading material with him so he would not have to yell back at me from across the living room. We had finally come to his family, and I was becoming more baffled by the moment. I could not keep the great-uncles straight and had difficulty figuring which great-aunt or -uncle belonged with which. I was finally down to a box of photos we had gotten from his mother when she was downsizing to move into a small apartment.

These were easier to identify. Old black-and-white photos of the farm, color prints of Gary and Galen at the farm, the farm in winter, the farm in summer, the wheat crop. And then I came to a photo that looked strange, like one of those pictures that seemed to have been snapped by accident. What I saw was an old pile of red metal, all bent up. I reached over to the trash bin and nearly tossed it in, but thought better of it.

"Hey," I called to Galen in the living room. "What's this one?" He sighed and came to the table, probably thinking it was another great-aunt or -uncle. He took the photo and flipped it over in his hand. He stared at it for a great while. His normally cheerful face seemed to fall into sadness. This accidental photo meant something to him.

"What is it?" I asked.

"That was the day my dad almost died," he said softly.

"What?" I had not been prepared for that answer. He stood over the table and laid the photo in front of both of us; he had not stopped looking at it. Then he sat down beside me.

"That's the tractor he was on that day. I don't know how it happened." He pointed to the photo. Now I could make out that it was a tractor. I could see a wheel, but the rest was a jumble of bends and breaks.

"That's the old tricycle tractor we had. I think it was a Case. It was an ancient one. I can't remember the year. I don't even know where Dad got it." He sat down at the kitchen table with me, his eyes not leaving the photo.

"This was taken up at the old place on the county line in Kiowa County. Gary and Dad and I were up there digging fenceposts. I was just a kid—I think I was ten or twelve. Dad was moving the tractor near the old silo, just to the west, and there was a gate—there."

He pointed to an area just beyond the white border of the photo, pushing at the border with his finger, as if to make it move just a little further out. The gate he had spoken of was just outside the frame.

"He had to go through the wash, and somehow it dug into the bank, and it had heaved up in the back. The frame bent, and the steering wheel had him pinned. It was still running. Dad was choking. I yelled at Gary, and he ran to the pickup to get help. I turned to Dad and jumped on the wheel."

"Wasn't that dangerous? "I asked.

"Yes. I mean, it was still running—but all I saw was Dad, and what I needed to do to stop it."

"How did you get it stopped?"

"The kill switch. I knew right where it was. You had to pull it to stop the tractor. The wheel was still churning through the dirt, and I climbed on it. It took me right where the switch was. But Dad was still choking, still pinned down. It was horrible. Horrible. Horrible."

"The engine stopped right away," he continued, "but the weight of the back of the tractor was still pressing down on Dad. I tried laying on my back; then I pushed with my feet. We had to get Dad down off it."

"Where was Gary?" I asked.

"He was there. We both pulled Dad down onto the ground. Then we took him to the hospital."

I stared at him, unable to speak.

Galen fixed his eyes on me now. His voice became sterner as he spoke.

"I know you might say, 'If it hadn't been for you,' or this or that. But I'm telling you, Amy, a lot had to line up for all that to come to pass."

I said nothing. I had never heard this event spoken of by Galen, Gary, or his parents. In fact, no one in the family had ever discussed it.

"Gary asked me years later if I remembered that day, and I said I did. He was still upset about it. He said Dad would have died if he had been alone with him."

"'You saved him'—that's what he told me," Galen continued. "I had to tell him that I couldn't tell Dad's story of the tractor without telling the bullfrog story first. They go together in my mind. Always have."

I had heard the bullfrog story before, but not the two stories together. Never. Yet, somehow, the two stories of the bullfrog and the tractor had been forever linked in Galen's mind. I was about to discover why.

"I fell into the stock tank there at the house," he began. Again, he pointed to a place far outside the white border of the photograph.

"I was looking at a bullfrog. Then I noticed how beautiful the water was."

Galen seemed to relax as he told his tale.

"The water in the tank was about three feet deep, and all green, with bright sunlight going through it. I don't know if I sensed I was drowning, but I certainly was. I don't remember if it mattered to me. I was calm. I was also a stupid little kid, about three. Kids that age don't know they're drowning or in danger. I was concentrating on that bullfrog and didn't realize I had fallen face first into that tank. My feet were tangled up in the weeds outside the tank. I couldn't back out."

"At first," he continued, "I tried to flail around and try to get out. When that didn't work, I just relaxed and went back to concentrating on that frog."

"Did you feel like you were dying?" I asked quietly.

"Well, I felt like I was leaving my body, you know, like it was floating up out of me."

"You were dying?"

"It seems that way now, but I didn't know it at the time. Yep. I think so. I know that I felt a sense of peace. I don't know how long I was in there; I have no idea. Gary seemed to come out of nowhere. He pulled me out. He saved my life." Galen looked away from the photo at last, and into my eyes. I stared back at him in disbelief.

"I was soaking wet. Mom was working in the garden, and when she saw me later, I got into trouble. I don't think Gary even told her I fell in. Go figure!" Again, he got quiet for a time.

"Somehow, both those memories of me in the stock tank and that tractor accident fit together," he began again. "I can't remember one without remembering the other. Both events, the bullfrog and the tractor, happened at different times in my life. About ten years apart, I think. And they both happened in that very yard, near the house."

"I told Gary the whole story not that long ago. Gary just stared at me. I told him he had saved my life when I was just a little guy.

'You saved me; I saved Dad. Everybody got a turn. We still had Dad at the end of the day.' That's what I told him."

After hearing Galen's story, one thing was clear: Gary had saved my husband's life. Because of Gary's quick action, I had a husband, we had daughters, and our daughters had a father and a grandfather. Because of Galen, my girls had a grandfather, and Galen and Gary still had their dad for many years. Our lives could have been very different were it not for the quick action of the two brothers, in separate events, nearly a decade apart, the events transpiring in a farmyard, only feet apart.

"That's exactly what happened. Gary did good," my husband finished and then wandered back into the living room. I suspected he wandered back to the memories of that day, and his dad. I gave him some space and did not follow him.

I sat and stared at the photo for a long time after Galen had left the dining room.

One picture.

Two separate events, happening decades apart, in nearly the exact same place.

Lives saved.

So many memories.

"Whatever happened to that tractor?" I finally called to him.

"It still ran! Dad and I put some new tires on it. We used it to dig postholes, and as a brush hog."

I shook my head. "Farmers," I muttered under my breath.

Some might say these events were random, just coincidences. I do not believe they were. God had everything to do with it. Both Gary and Galen had choices to make on those separate days that had determined their futures; that was true. Their choices had determined all our futures.

"I think I found a word for what happened with you and your brother with the bullfrog and the tractor!" I said to him, weeks later. I was looking up the definition of a word and came across the word by accident. "It's called a *concatenation*."[2] I had practiced pronouncing it properly all day, and then I spelled it.

He looked up from a parts catalogue he was reading. "Did you make that up?"

"Nope. It's Latin!"

"Where did you get it?" He seemed suspicious.

"The dictionary, Galen. It means a series of events that are related or linked together."

"I like the bullfrog and the tractor better," he responded, smiling.

That night as we were getting ready for bed, he began to talk about his father.

"I miss Dad. I did for a long time, even before he died."

Carl had been ill and unable to help Galen on the farm any longer. To say that he missed him was an understatement. They had worked together all Galen's life.

"When he got sick and wasn't able to come out and help anymore because of his dialysis, everything changed for me. I had come to rely on Dad, and he on me. I had others help out, but it wasn't the same. He was my partner; we did everything together."

Finally, just before he fell asleep, I heard him ask me a question.

"What do they call that?"

"Love, Galen. They call that love."

8

The Woman on the Sofa

The tempest comes out from its chamber, the cold from the driving winds. The breath of God produces ice, and the broad waters become frozen. He loads the clouds with moisture; he scatters his lightning through them. At his direction they swirl around over the face of the whole earth to do whatever he commands them. He brings the clouds to punish people, or to water his earth and show his love. (Job 37:9–13 NIV)

We pulled up in the drive next to the old white house. It was small and looked as if it were held together by a few nails, some tar paper, and a whole lot of prayer. But the rent was cheap, and we were desperate. We had left the farm when Galen's dad, Carl, fell seriously ill and could no longer partner him in the business. My husband had taken a job with a local poultry producer. I had managed to get a position with a local nursing home. That was how we had found our way to the little town many miles away from the farm Galen had grown up on. Galen soon found a more permanent job in a nearby factory, as well as the opportunity to attend college to add to his bachelor's degree in biology. The field he had chosen was a good one, working in the water industry, with many job possibilities.

The school would even assist him in seeking employment following his graduation. Galen was at work until well past midnight at the factory, and often worked overtime, which meant he would arrive home after midnight most nights, sleep, and then wake up and be at school the entire day. It made for long, busy days for him. Our daughter, Sarah and I were left to ourselves quite a bit of time in the evenings.

Shortly after Galen had started school and his new job at the factory, I had found myself feeling ill. Several years before we had moved from the farm, I had had two miscarriages. I found I was miscarrying again. Heartbroken, and with so many demands on our finances and time, I returned to work earlier than the doctor advised, but I discovered I was not able to lift, nor stand on my feet for long periods of time. Eventually, I lost my job. I had known the pain of miscarriage before, but this was different. During the other miscarriages, I had cried and prayed to God for comfort. He had been there, increasing my faith and soothing my broken heart. But this time seemed different. I did not know what was going on. My grief seemed more complicated this time.

Our life had become more complicated. Whatever money we had was going out to utilities, rent on the old house, and other indebtedness from our move from the farm. There was very little left over for food, and absolutely nothing for anything frivolous. We had a small truck and a car, which we were paying monthly payments on. Within a few months, the car was repossessed. For a time, we went on assistance, which allowed us a voucher to get free milk, peanut butter, cheese, bread, cereal, and vegetables. In addition to a peanut butter sandwich, Sarah and I made a meal of our potato each night. Sometimes we would sprinkle cheese on it. I had counted each potato and each slice of bread so that we could make our larder last at least two weeks. Sarah would eat and then go outside to play with the neighborhood children. Later, I would wrap one of my favorite aprons around her tiny waist, and we would wash dishes together.

We soon noticed an array of things wrong with the inside of the house. We walked into the bathroom one day to find that the toilet had fallen through the rotten floor and now lay on the dirt beneath the floor. The following day, we found a few old pieces of wood and blocked and covered the floor with a piece of plywood that we had found in the old shed. After a large rainstorm not long after that, we noticed a steady stream of water coming out of our small linen closet. We relocated our things out of the tiny linen cabinet and did not use it. A five-gallon bucket was discovered outside the back-porch door. It did not take me long to put it to use each time it rained. In the kitchen, we used an old pot that we placed in the center of the kitchen, where most of the drips seemed to be falling. Leaks had also infiltrated behind the walls of the living room and had made the wood paneling permanently ripple in places. Complaints to our landlord fell on deaf ears.

Winter entered quietly into our lives, just after Sarah and I had gotten our routine down in tending to the rain showers. Now it was just cold. There was no central heat, or air. We had a small stack of quilts; nearly each of them would go on Sarah at night. I had a small electric heater, which I would run at night. I placed it in the kitchen, facing Sarah's room to keep her and hopefully the kitchen pipes from freezing at night. It seemed to work well.

It was winter when the dream came. It seemed so real.

I could feel the breeze blowing my hair and the blades of grass between my toes. I was walking on a carpet of green that stretched up to a low-rising hill. I seemed to know where I was going, but I could not recall ever having been there before. It was lovely. I came to the crest of the hill, and I saw them; there were children, and they were playing. The giggles and noises they made caught my attention, and I stopped and watched them for a time. I felt myself smile in my dream. It felt so foreign, that smile. I hadn't smiled in a very long time in the awake world. My face had seemed for a moment to have forgotten how it felt.

I watched the children; each was a different age but still quite young. They were holding hands and playing and laughing together. Suddenly, they saw me. They stopped and smiled at me. Then they lined up before me. They looked so familiar, as if they might be family. Two boys and two girls? I don't recall, but I knew instantly that they were mine. But how? Finally, I asked the question that had been burning in my heart since I first saw them: "Whose children are these?" I called aloud.

I awoke at the sound of my own voice. I looked over to see Galen asleep next to me. Sweat beads were thick on my face, and my hair was matted with dampness. I slipped out from the covers and into the bathroom, running cool water into my cupped hands. I splashed water on my face and neck. I knew it had been a dream, but I could still hear the children, and see their faces when I closed my eyes. Minutes passed, and soon it all faded away. I lifted the little curtain that covered the bathroom window. The branches of the Rose of Sharon bush lay bare in the chilly wind outside and were heavy with ice. I looked in on Sarah. She was sleeping soundly beneath the high piles of quilts. I managed to return to bed and fall back into a fitful sleep. Once Sarah was off to school, I thought again of the dream and what it might have meant. Was it simply normal grieving? My life seemed to be coming unhemmed, and I felt helpless to repair it. In fact, I began to blame myself for all failures that our family was suffering. A hopeless settled over me. The dream and all it had brought with it could not have come at a worse time, I thought. Didn't God understand my heart was broken?

We had endured plenty of storms in the past, both spiritual and physical ones. God had been there during all of them. Where was He? Why was this one different? Were we out of His will? It was then that I had to confess, if only to myself, that my peace had been shattered when we had to leave our farm. I could not deny it. But as I looked out to the horizon as we headed away from our life there, I had a hope, a sensing that God had it all under control. Had I believed it? Or was it simple wishful praying? I stood in the cold kitchen one night, opening lower cupboards and hoping to avoid a broken pipe beneath the sink, and came to a startling conclusion: God had taken away our farm and our life, and now He was taking away my peace and my hope of a family. Yes, He had put us into this situation where we had to depend solely upon Him, without the comfort of family or familiar surroundings. He had removed every prop out from under me, everything I had clung to since leaving the farm. I had no job and no prospects, our lives were in a rush heading somewhere ... and I sensed that. I was simply unable to see where. My attempts to keep it all in perspective were threadbare.

One of the last times I had been to church, I was approached by a lady who told me how sorry she was that I had miscarried.

"But you know, a good apple doesn't fall off the tree," she said, patting my arm.

My heart and spirit felt trampled by her as she walked away, unaware of the harm and wounding she had added to me. I stared after her, and another woman came to me saying she had been praying for me. I nodded in acknowledgement. I hoped she would have better luck that I was having. I was weary from my waiting for God to answer even one of my prayers. Surely it could not have been plainer that I was saddened, eager to hear from Him, and in need of comfort. Slowly I resigned myself to never hearing from Him and stopped praying altogether. He had abandoned us here in this place, I reasoned. And without realizing it at the time, my faith and all I had always clung to were as dead and dry as the Rose of Sharon bush outside our bathroom window. Leaving church that day, I sat in the parking lot and opened my Bible, hoping to find a bit of comfort. It opened immediately to the book of Job. I slammed it shut at once. I was not ready for any of that! Surrounded by what I felt were ill-advised people who claimed to be his friends, Job had to endure not only their prattling but the feeling of being abandoned by God. The darkness of that abyss I looked into now and then began to see as appealing. So bottomless, so dark, almost secure. I stood before it one day, waiting for something to happen. Perhaps I would simply fall into it and vanish without a trace.

I almost did.

It was still winter—the first weeks of January. Winter had seemed to last for years, and ice continued to coat everything outside. I had taken to sleeping on the sofa some nights. The television would be on, and I saw it without seeing it; the voices from it seemed to drone on and on, making no sense to me. I lay there one night wrapped in an afghan, found the old black-and-white movie channel, and rested my head on the armrest of the sofa. I fell asleep almost at once and awakened just as quickly. It was three in the morning. The movie was gone, replaced by a man whose eyes were tightly shut in prayer. He was praying for someone—a woman, I thought I heard—as I turned the channel to the news.

Once Sarah and Galen were gone for the day, I sat down on the sofa, pondering the dark pit that I felt I had fallen into. The sides seemed so slippery that I doubted that I could ever climb out. It seemed as if God had abandoned me. I settled back into the morning news program and realized that the news was not on. It was that praying man again! I sat up straighter and listened.

"There's a woman. You are crying. There is deep grief. You've suffered loss, death."

The praying man seemed so sincere, so persistent to reach her, whoever she was. I turned the channel back to the news. Still, I felt sorry for the woman whom I had already heard about twice now. Whoever she was, I had a feeling I knew how she felt.

That evening, Sarah and I had finished watching a movie. I turned the television off and began her nightly routine of brushing teeth, going to the bathroom, and snuggling under her mountain of quilts. As I aimed the little room heater toward her room and shut the lights off, I heard a noise in the living room. I thought I had turned the television off. I was in disbelief when I returned to see the praying man on television again, praying the same prayer, for the same poor woman! I headed toward the television and started to turn it off when the man began speaking earnestly.

"Please, please, listen to me!" This was not quite the same as he had prayed before. His eyes were tightly closed, and he was so intent on getting this woman's attention that I stopped and sat on the sofa to listen to him.

"There's a woman, and you're sitting on a sofa. You're wearing a housedress. You have been in such deep grief and loss. Something has been taken from you. Please—listen! The Lord wants you to know that He is going to restore that to you."

This was the third time in the past two days I had heard the praying man plead with the woman on the sofa to hear him. I looked down at the pink flowered flannel housedress I was wearing, dumbfounded. Was it me? And if so, what was God going to restore to me?

I slept soundly that night, not hearing when Galen came in or when he arose to leave for school. When Sarah was safely on her way to school, I went to the kitchen and checked a few dates on the calendar. I sat there for a moment or two on the sofa, disbelieving what I felt might be true. Was I pregnant? Had God been trying to tell me all this time, and I had tuned Him out? It took me nearly two weeks to get the courage to do a pregnancy test. The results, which should have filled me with dread because of my previous history, made me stand up and begin to dance in that old kitchen. As the morning light streamed in through the little kitchen window, I laughed and cried and danced. After months of depression, fear, anger, and hopelessness, I felt myself begin to hope. I turned on the Christian station nearly every day after that, hoping to her more of the woman on the sofa, but he never mentioned her again. Not ever. He did not have to. I knew the woman on the sofa was me. That August, we had a beautiful baby girl, Laura. There was not a single difficulty with the pregnancy, nor the birth.

Miracles continued to flow in our lives in other ways, as well. At the completion of Galen's coursework, a job offer presented itself.

We could not stop praising God. We had relocated to the east coast. One of my first items of business was to get Sarah enrolled in school that year. She had to have a physical and her shot records updated. I had taken her to a family doctor recommended by one of Galen's new coworkers, near where we lived. I had gone to her earlier that week to meet her and see if she would be a good fit for our family. I signed papers to release my records to her, as well as Laura's and Sarah's. She had already received my file from my previous doctor, and it sat on top of her desk.

"You are so lucky to have Sarah," the doctor said, handing me the little paper folder containing her shot records and stroking Sarah's head.

"She is a good girl." I nodded. "She's been really excited about moving and her new baby sister."

The doctor looked up at me. She walked behind her desk and grabbed a file that lay there. It was my file. She pulled out a yellow sheet and perused it. She explained they were lab results from my last visit to my own doctor before we had moved. She looked over at me as if she were about to explain something very difficult to someone very young.

"No," she said; her head shook slightly.

"No?" I parroted.

"I mean you are lucky you have Sarah because she is the only one you will ever have."

She held up a slip of yellow paper with lab results on it. "This is the lab results from your doctor."

I looked at it. On it was my doctor's letterhead, and lab results. A big question mark was penned in red ink across one side of it, meaning he was as confused at the lab results as I currently was. What did that mean?

"I don't know how to tell you this, but you have already gone through menopause. There's no physical way you could get pregnant, nor carry a baby to term. It's just impossible."

I stood up, walked to the door, and called for Galen. He was carrying Laura. The doctor shook her head, completely confused, and then took Laura from Galen's arms.

"Well, you have a miracle baby, and that's for sure," she said, cooing at Laura. "And I guess I have another new patient."

Galen and I just smiled.

Years later, we would finally move back to the Midwest, and eventually back to our little town. I asked Galen to drive me back to the old house we had once lived in. I was saddened as we rounded the corner and discovered it had been completely torn down.

"Thank God!" My husband was jubilant.

I did not feel that way. I asked him to turn down the alley at the back of the lot, and I got out. Most of the rubble had been hauled away, but there were bits of it everywhere. I stood there in the now-vacant lot, not knowing exactly why I wanted to be there. The last time I had stood there, I had had a seven-year-old and a newborn. Sarah had grown up and was now a mother herself. She had gone to college, getting a degree in office management. On the day that Laura was born, the nurse had gone into the waiting room and gotten Sarah. She gowned her up, wrapping her much as I had wrapped her in the apron when we did the dishes together in the old house. She gave her a clean, warm cloth when she helped the nurse give Laura her first bath. The nurse told me later it was the most precious thing she had ever seen and the first time she had ever done it.

I looked at the place where the clothesline had been and at the crumbly foundation where the old shed had been. Many things we had brought with us from the farm had been stored there: my wedding dress, books from my college days, papers, some photographs, small bits of life we had wanted to remember from our days at the farm. Most of those items had been destroyed by water damage and mold. We had been away for many years, and in that time, I had come to think of the place where I stood as almost holy in some way. I looked around, recalling the devastation the house had wrought on our belongings and the sadness I had felt there, as well as the joy.

Holy? How could I ever have thought of this place as a holy place? This place, with its rippled walls and water pouring out of the linen cupboard with each storm? How could a sinking toilet be holy? The answer for me was a simple one: to me, it was where God had come and where angels had danced with me in the tiny kitchen.

In his book *The Rational Bible*, Dennis Prager's commentary on Exodus 3:5 brought me clarity:

> Of course, this random spot in some wilderness is not inherently holy. It is holy because God appears there. Any place or situation into which we bring God or where we encounter God ... becomes holy.[1]

Laura went on to complete her teaching credential in elementary education. Before settling in to teach kindergarten in the States, she took a job in South Korea for a year, where she worked as a teacher in a private school. One night, I received an email from her:

> I didn't want to join in prayer time at church. We get together in groups of 3 or 4 and pray for each other. The two Korean ladies that sat in front of me were friends so I was the oddball in the group. I felt encouraged as we prayed, and I got to encourage one of the ladies. This woman had a miscarriage the year before and she was starting to feel scared that she would never be able to conceive. After we prayed together, I took her hands and told her I had an encouragement for her. I gave her a brief synopsis of our family history and how God brought restoration in the end. She was overjoyed and she and her friend kept going, "Amen! Amen! Miracle baby!" I was glad I was able to encourage her.

One day, a friend of ours was listening to me share a bit about those difficult times, and he pulled me aside.

"Just hear me out on something," he began. "You have always thought of Laura's birth as supernatural, and because of that you feel she is special. Which she is! But I'd like to throw something out for you to think about, because I believe it's true. He didn't do that for Laura—He did that for you, Amy. God did that for you."

I had a problem understanding that for a very long time, much as I had a problem understanding God's unconditional love for me. At first, I protested at my friend's comments. Surely, all the losses I had before Laura's birth, the praying man on the television, the flawless pregnancy and birth that followed, and ending with the physician telling me it was impossible for me to even have had her at all—those things taken together pointed to Laura being special in some way. Sort of akin to being the lone survivor of a plane crash. Of course, to her father and sister and myself, she most certainly was a gift, a blessing, and a miracle.

When I have given a gift to someone, all the glory has belonged to me, the giver. And then there are gifts that come from God. God's gifts are those we do not keep—we share. This experience has become part of my testimony. I have shared them, marveled at them, recalled them with great joy and gladness. That is part of my testimony. I had looked upon myself all those years as the caretaker of a miracle. Nothing more. But there was more to the story. Much more. Part of what God had been attempting to teach me had finally been revealed when Laura had prayed with that woman at church in South Korea. My dear friend had been right: I was not only the caretaker of a miracle; I had been the recipient of a miracle.

I had nearly finished my brief walk through the shards of old brick and wood siding when my eye caught on a flat piece of dirty white Formica scattered with little gold flecks. It bore several deep cut marks, like those of a knife. I wondered—had those been my cut marks when Sarah and I were feasting on our nightly potato? Maybe so. I picked it up to save it, my heart full, and my tears came freely.

Then Job replied to the LORD: "I know that you can do all things; no purpose of yours can be thwarted. You asked, 'Who is this that obscures my plans without knowledge?' Surely I spoke of things I did not understand, things too wonderful for me to know. You said, 'Listen now, and I will speak; I will question you, and you shall answer me.' My ears had heard of you but now my eyes have seen you. Therefore I despise myself and repent in dust and ashes." (Job 40:1–6 NIV)

The gift I had received went beyond carrying a child. His gift to me was His presence, His forgiveness, His peace, and the knowledge that storms come, and He is there in the midst of them. In this dirt-filled lot, with remnants of destruction all around me, I realized He had not been distant or aloof, but working right there all the time, stronger than any storm I had faced, or would face. I had always thought it, but now, I knew it. I was reminded of Job. I believe I understood him a bit better.

$$9$$

The Dream

Every experience God gives us, every person He puts in our lives, is the perfect preparation for the future that only He can see.[1]

"I can't believe you gave up a job as a nurse to type. Weren't you a good nurse?"

Those were the first words Sarah ever spoke to me. I had taken a break from nursing and found a temporary job with a medical transcription agency. It was there that I first met Sarah.

Loud, brash, abrasive. She had bragged only moments earlier to a coworker about being tossed out of a bar the night before for arguing with the bartender. She continued to glare at me, expecting some sort of response to the question she had directed my way. She flipped a lock of bleached blond hair away from her face, revealing crystal-blue eyes. Those icy eyes appraised my face, leaving me with the feeling that I was undergoing an x-ray. I excused myself from the small table we were sitting at and returned to my transcription machine. I could hear Sarah's hearty laugh echo down the hall. I did not know if she was laughing at me.

I had heard about Sarah before I met her. Jo, the office manager, spoke candidly to me during my job interview, and later during my orientation to the office, about her. By the ease of her speech, it was clear that Jo's speech about Sarah was well-rehearsed and given to all new hires. Basically, I was advised discreetly to avoid her.

"I keep her on because she is an excellent typist, and one or two of our clients are very fond of her," Jo concluded in her thick southern drawl.

I watched as the little group of coworkers who had been with me earlier in the break room had found their ways back to their desks, and the *tat-tat-tat* of keyboard strokes filled the air once again. I sat down at my desk, still a bit rattled by my first encounter with Sarah. I heard a voice come from directly behind me. It was Lynn.

"Don't let Sarah get to you," she whispered without missing a single keystroke. "If there's one thing you should know about Sarah, it's that she's really a big softy." *Oh Lord,* I thought, *really?* I was not convinced.

I was grateful when Janice was hired. Quiet, with a sweet disposition, she was pleasant to talk to, and I enjoyed our breaks together and getting to know her. Janice was feminine, efficient, quiet, and kind—attributes that Sarah did not even pretend to possess. Every time Sarah's icy blue stare caught sight of Janice in the hall or going to the manager's office, Sarah seemed to bristle and mutter things under her breath.

"I don't know what I am doing wrong," Janice confided to me one day. "What did I do to make her dislike me?"

"Nothing." I did not know how else to respond. "It takes her time to warm up to people, I guess. Lynn said she is really a softy." I added that last bit, and Janice's eyes told me she did not believe it any more than I had.

Sarah wasn't at her usual desk one Monday morning, and I felt the mood in the office lift brightly. But Tuesday came, and then Wednesday and Thursday, and no Sarah. Lynn finally told us that Sarah had gone to a doctor's appointment, and some tests had been ordered. She assured us that she would return to work Friday, sometime after lunch. Sure enough, at about 1:00 p.m., Sarah arrived, electric with anger about one thing or another. My initial concern for her slowly evaporated as the day went on. The happy, restful ambiance of our office was now a memory. Sarah stormed up the middle aisle toward her desk. Then, as she passed me, she stopped briefly and leaned over my shoulder.

"You're going on break with me," she hissed in my ear.

It was not an invitation; it was a command. Janice's eyebrows vanished beneath her bangs. She had heard.

At breaktime, I followed Sarah, who was marching purposefully down the hall toward the ladies' lounge.

"You're a nurse, right?" I nodded. To be honest, being there with Sarah made me feel uncomfortable. But with that feeling came another: the sense that God had placed this angry, wayward girl in front of me and forced me to look and not turn away from her. She had come into my life for a purpose. I just did not know what that purpose was.

"Well, let me ask you something," she continued. "If someone came into your office you were working in, wouldn't you look at their chart at least once?" I was certain it wasn't a question, but I nodded all the same.

"I want you to look at this and tell me if I look like a candidate for a bilateral mammogram," she finished angrily. And without another word, Sarah lifted her loose-fitting shirt up. I noted a long, well-healed scar where her right breast should have been disappearing up under an empty cup of her bra.

"Amy, I waited there three hours, and they had me confused with someone else, and then they didn't even do a mammogram on the good one I have left!"

We sat in the lounge for the entire break by ourselves and talked. She explained that she had been diagnosed with breast cancer at the age of twenty-four. Now, at the age of twenty-six, she said her specialist believed the cancer had returned.

Over a period of the next two months, Lynn and I managed to finally talk Sarah into going back and having the mammogram done on the remaining breast as a precaution. The doctor followed up with a brief hospitalization, which included a complete physical work-up, more blood work, and x-rays. A bone scan was performed. All were clear. No sign of the cancer. Sarah immediately wanted to throw a big party, and we were all relieved. She confided to me that she would often take her days off and weekends to go to the hospital and visit with women who were facing radical surgeries, as she had. She had become a cancer coach.

Winter appeared, first with showers of sleet pelting our building's windows, and then the snow came, thick and heavy. Many of the girls did not make it to work due to the weather, including Sarah. It became noticeable that Sarah did not seem to be bouncing back from her ordeal of the past fall, despite her clean bill of health. If anything, she looked weak, and she had lost a lot of weight. Lynn thought she had been dieting. Sarah herself did not say much. Finally, Lynn told us the news that Sarah could not.

"It's back. All those tests and they missed it." And then she received even more heartbreaking news. "She's been trying to get back with her little girl, and things have been going so well. Now this has happened! And I don't know …" Lynn's voice trailed off.

Sarah felt well enough to work until the fall the following year, and into the next winter. Near the Christmas holiday, we all had a chance to work some overtime for extra cash. I was working late and alone in the office when Sarah appeared in the doorway. She was working only half days now. Sitting for long periods of time had become painful for her. We watched as she would frequently stand and stretch and take short walks up and down the hallway between long transcriptions. Sometimes she would heave and not return at all. She came to my desk and sat down in the aisle across from my desk and faced me.

"Amy, you aren't going to believe the dream I had," she began. I stopped typing. "I don't want you to think I'm crazy or something, but I think I am getting ready to die."

The dream, she said, had been a recurring one. It had begun

about the time she was told her cancer had returned, over a year earlier.

"I was making funeral arrangements and cleaning the house and laying out the clothes I was going to be buried in."

I sat in silence. I really did not know what to say.

"And now this!" Sarah stood and pointed all over her body. "Amy, it's everywhere! It's even in my bones!"

Sarah sat back down and, after a time, spoke again.

"I was in my apartment in my dream," she continued. "I found this room I had never been in. So I went inside to have a look around. There was a casket, and the top was open. I walked up to it. I was in that coffin! I stared at myself for the longest time. It was funny, like seeing myself for the first time. I heard a noise behind me and realized that Dennie had come into the room and come up behind me. I told her she could not be there and she could not follow me. She had a life to life and things to do."

There were no tears. There was only a confused, unfocused gaze as she stared back into her dream.

"As I am talking to her, I am looking back at myself in that coffin."

Silence.

"I know it sounds like I'm giving up," she finally said. "I guess you think I should fight this. But I am tired. I must tell Dennie, and I just don't know what to do. She doesn't really know me. We were just getting to know each other."

Sarah's voice grew faint and then stopped altogether. Finally, she began to cry. I did, too.

"Why would God do this to me?" she asked. And with those words, I took Sarah's hand, and we began the longest walk of her young life. I had become a part of her journey. I wanted her to know she wasn't by herself. God was there, and friends. We would all go on this journey together with her.

I left the office that night during a snowstorm. As the snow fell, I prayed. I prayed for Sarah. I prayed for her little daughter, Dennie.

I prayed for myself, that God would give me a tangible task to do for them both. I felt frustrated, disappointed, and brokenhearted about Sarah's life.

"It's not supposed to work this way," I called out to God at a stoplight. "Don't you know she has a little girl?" Of course, He did.

I prayed that God would spare her life and asked Him repeatedly to give her strength. It was too much to comprehend that she was so sick and had so much life ahead of her.

Winter passed, and then spring came. Sarah seemed to have rallied. The long, humid southern summer had begun. With her radiation and chemo appointments, Sarah had no longer been able to come to work and had taken an extended leave of absence. Finally, she resigned. Some of us girls took shifts visiting her at her apartment, and when we did, we were greeted at the door with the usual stories and jokes.

"How are things with you and Dennie?" I asked on one of my visits. She smiled and pointed over at two small, framed photos resting on her bedside table. Both had been taken at a beach. Her eyes scanned the photos; her voice softened.

"Wish I had more time. I did my best to make some memories."

"Well, I am glad I had time with you, and that you didn't manage to run me away from my job!" I blurted out. She stared at me for a moment, and her face broke into a wide smile.

"Yeah, you just hung in there with me. You must have known me better than I thought!" she replied.

I grinned back and said nothing. Sarah's expression sobered.

"I guess I didn't think you would understand my life. It's different than yours. There hasn't been much to be happy about. I really made a mess of things."

"You really think any of us in this world has a perfect life? I haven't, and no one I know has. We are all on a journey, Sarah." I shared a bit of my testimony with her, including my miscarriages and other disappointing times. I don't know how long we sat there and talked. When I finished, she continued to stare at me.

"I never knew that," she offered quietly.

I had attempted to speak with her about salvation many times, but she held up her hands, rebuffing me with each attempt I made. I must have had that *I'm going to bring up God* look, because Sarah focused those crystal-blue eyes on me.

"I think I know you pretty well." She smirked at me. "I know what you are going to say! And it's funny that you would bring it up!"

I stared at her. I hadn't said a word. Her smirk faded a bit.

"You won't believe who came by the ICU last time I was there at the hospital. My old preacher! We talked, and I understand some things I didn't before."

She went on to say, in an uncharacteristically quiet voice, that she had rededicated her life to God. Sarah looked at me in the strangest way at that point, as if to ask if her efforts might be too little, too late, or if her rededication might be invalid, somehow.

"I am neither shocked nor surprised at you coming to your senses at last!" I said jovially, hugging her gently. Her smile immediately returned, and her eyes sparkled. Sarah had found Him again. He had helped her get her earthly house in order. In the quiet of that tiny apartment filled with the smell of death, I saw peace in those crystal-blue eyes for the first time.

Several months later, a phone call came. We had recently relocated back to the Midwest, and had barely finished moving in. It was Janice. It was a phone call I had been waiting for.

"You know I visited her in the ICU. That happened about a week before you left. I need to tell you that Sarah and I got close during that time. Can you believe it?" She paused. "Well, as close as she ever allowed anyone.

"She died last night, Amy. Dennie was right there at her bedside. Sarah stayed at peace right to the end. I thought you would like to know that." I waited for a few moments to pass before I thanked her.

My thoughts drifted back to the last time I had seen Sarah. We parted, knowing it would be for the last time. I drove slowly past her apartment as I left. Lynn was staying with her off and on and had placed the hospital bed by the big window in the living room. I saw her sit up and wave, a smile on her weary face. It must have taken all her strength to do that.

That night, after Janice's call, I thought of Sarah's dream. The dream had shown her what would come, but it carried with it a gift: Time. Somehow, peace would come to her; she had made memories with her daughter and had found God again. God had given her that time. There was also the matter of her friends, who had stood with her and helped her realize that she was loved and accepted just the way she was. I thought of one of my many talks I had had with Sarah about God. I had told her that when I got to heaven, I would like to look out and see her there. That would make me happy, I had told her. I believe that when that day does come, I will see her. All I will have to do is look for those icy-blue eyes. I am certain I will recognize her.

10

The Big House

He heals the brokenhearted and binds up their
wounds.

—Psalm 147:3 (NIV)

I was traveling more frequently to see Momma following her heart
surgery, taking her to doctor's appointments and running business
errands for her. My favorite time with her was sharing in her church
family. I had come to think of it as my own as my visits grew more
frequent and of longer duration.

It had been a normal Sunday morning. We arrived, and Momma
went right away to her favorite seat. I followed along, and as I was
about to sit down, a lady in a brightly colored blouse walked past
me and gently squeezed my hand. It was Diane. In a moment she
was gone, and I caught a glimpse of her on stage, where she sang as
part of the worship team.

After service, I headed down the aisle and turned to find that
Momma had not been beside me. Instead, she was standing at the
pew we had shared, blocked from moving into the aisle by Diane
and deep in conversation with her. Presently, Momma broke away
from her. She wove slowly through the crowded aisle, where people
had stopped to visit following the service, and as she passed me, she

grabbed my arm. Hurriedly, she maneuvered me toward the front doors of the church and out into the parking lot. Finally, when we were in the car, I asked what was going on.

"Oh, it's that Diane again. She wants me to come and eat dinner Friday night at her place, and she wants me to bring you, too." She was quiet for a moment and then added, "I have flat run out of excuses to make."

"Her place? Doesn't she live in the big house?"

"Yes."

"And what did you tell her?"

"I told her we would," she stated, resignedly.

Friday came, and we pulled down the drive to Diane's place and parked.

"Welcome!" Diane greeted us happily and at the top of her voice the moment we had opened the car doors. We made our way up the brick pathway; Momma lingered for a time at the entrance.

"I really don't want to be here," she whispered to me. "I really want to go home."

Momma was quiet and unassuming, while Diane was loud and loved to be in the middle of everything. They mixed about as well as the proverbial oil and water. Perhaps that was her reluctance at accepting the invitation.

I had never been in the house since it had been finished. To my knowledge, neither had Momma. Nor had I had ever seen what I had always called the big house furnished inside. In fact, the last time I had been in it was as a little girl, just after the living room had been carpeted. This house, the big house, had been built by my father. It was to have been our house. We had never lived in it, however.

We entered the house and came immediately into the spacious living area. My eyes were drawn at once to the large picture window. Across the small valley dotted with live oaks and avocado trees, I could see the little house where I had grown up. The carpet and the paint seemed different to me. Of course, I reasoned to myself, it would have changed through the years. There had been at least four owners since my father had built it. My eyes scanned the walls decorated with artwork and photographs of Diane's family. They seemed out of place to me. I had always thought of the house as ours, even though we had never lived in it.

Diane insisted on a grand tour. We followed her from room to room. There were four bedrooms upstairs. The two bedrooms that that faced northwest would have belonged to myself and my sister, Beth. We would have shared a wide balcony, painted creamy white. From that balcony, we could look over the valley to the house we had been raised in. I followed behind Diane, who had my momma's arm wrapped in hers. I wandered through bathrooms, other bedrooms, and hallways, all familiar and all foreign. To me, this place represented an unrealized dream, a failed experiment. It had come to be a reminder to me of loss and sadness.

I recalled, as a young girl, being fascinated by the comings and goings at the house. Other people lived there. At night, the lights at the big house would glow and twinkle and nearly always caught my attention. I would sit on the bed, pull the curtains aside, and look out at it, across the valley. There were many family gatherings, with parades of cars going in and out through the years. Holidays would come and go, and the house would be bright and busy with activity. At times, I would imagine what it might have been like, to have lived in the big house. It would be a long time before I finally stopped looking across the valley at the big house.

Diane led us back downstairs for a brief tour of the main floor and then into the spacious kitchen, where she busied herself with the final preparations for dinner.

"I hope you like stew!" She grabbed stacks of bowls and small plates off the counter. "Come on, sit in here. It'll be done in a bit."

We wandered into the dining room. Diane remained in the kitchen while Momma leaned against the wall and stared out the windows that filled the wall next to a long dining table. I wondered what Momma had been thinking, as I had been lost in my own remembrances since we had entered the house.

"You two are being awfully quiet." It was Diane. "Why haven't you made yourselves at home? Come on and sit down," she insisted. She pulled a chair out for Momma, who obediently sat, facing the windows, which gave her an unobstructed view of the entire valley. Diane chatted nonstop as she ladled stew out to each of us and passed over a plate piled with thick slices of freshly baked bread.

"Hope it all tastes as good as it smells!" she called to us from the kitchen, where she had gone to put the pot of stew back on a burner to keep it warm. A phone rang from somewhere; I heard Diane walk down to the end of the kitchen and turn a corner, and I remembered from our tour that she had used a room off the kitchen as a small office. Momma remained strangely quiet, her eyes fixed on a corner near the dining table. Through the windows, I could see our little house.

"I was painting that piece of trim."

I looked over at Momma, who had pointed her finger at a spot near one of the windows, where she had been looking. Her voice sounded as if she were far away.

"Right there, on that ledge. Your dad walked in and said he wanted a divorce. I was on a ladder, there in the corner. I got down, and the paintbrush was still in my hand. I put it down. And I walked out of this house, and that was the end of my marriage."

I was stunned. I felt a bit disoriented by the memories and feelings the house seemed to have evoked that night in the both of us. Momma took further advantage of Diane's absence to speak again in a hushed tone.

"That was it," she finished. It was as if she had been wanting to say this for a very long time.

It swiftly became apparent why Momma had been so reluctant to come to Diane's house. I had never heard Momma speak of that day before. I stared over at her until Diane returned to the table. We finished the delicious stew and had pie for dessert. I was grateful that Diane was the sort who did not like silence and filled each quiet moment with chatter of some kind. We lingered long enough for a second cup of coffee, thanked Diane, and made our way down the lane, back to Momma's home.

"I'm really glad that's over with," she said once we had cleared the red rock road and turned onto the main road. She sounded exhausted. When we got home, she walked slowly toward her bedroom. I heard her brushing her teeth in the bathroom, and soon her bedroom light turned off.

"Good night," she called down the hall to me.

That night, I dreamed of Mrs. Berg, my third-grade teacher. I had not thought of her in years, yet there she was, standing in front of the class. She had been reading something to us from a textbook. She stopped, looked up from the book, and then plainly and loudly shouted, "Duck!" Of course, we all knew what to do. Books scattered everywhere, pencils skittered across the floor, and notebooks slid across the desks. We dropped to the floor at once, wriggled beneath each of our desks, covered our necks and faces with our hands, and closed our eyes tightly. We were not afraid, however. We did this every week.

Harry S. Truman's Federal Civil Defense Administration had deemed the drills as educational. It was meant to prepare us for something that might be possible, or might be inevitable. The menace they were trying to prepare and protect us from was an attack by atomic bomb. As children, we had all seen the grainy, black-and-white newsreels of Hiroshima and Nagasaki. But that was far away from us. We all thought it was great fun, sliding down on the floor, hiding beneath our desks like we were in our own little forts. But the teachers, principals, school boards, and parents had taken it quite seriously. The adults, it seemed to us kids, seemed to have prepared us for anything.

Everything, except divorce.

I was to discover that there had not been a desk large enough for me to hide beneath. The long tables that had lined the back of the classroom were not strong enough to shield me from that blast. My eyes had not been able to close tightly enough, nor were my arms strong enough to protect me from the damage caused by the bright, white light of the explosion that occurred and the debris that had fallen everywhere around me following my parents' divorce. I had felt defenseless, trapped, exposed. In my dream, I tried to recall the instructions Mrs. Berg had given us. She told us if we found ourselves out in the open, we must find an adult who would tell us what to do and where to go to be safe. But there had been no one.

When I awoke the next morning, my thoughts had become more distinct. I realized that Momma had never detailed what had transpired that day at the big house, when she and my father had agreed to divorce. After hearing her words, I began to see how her memories stirred during the evening at the big house dovetailed with my own memories as a child of the day my father left us. I had few memories of him, but I recalled those clearly.

My father had gone to the house that day to finish painting the trim in the kitchen. Momma had been helping him. I had come home from school; my younger sisters were away at a sitter so Momma could work at the big house. The unexpected presence of my father delighted me. I had hoped to see if he would take me back to the big house with him. I wanted to see what it looked like. But I continued to watch as he silently disappeared onto the back porch. There were a washer, a dryer, and shelves for storage back there. Of course, I followed him. I pushed the door open. He had reached to the top shelf, pushed some boxes aside, and found an old gray duffel bag.

"Where are you going?" I asked.

He did not look at me. "I have to go away."

He left the back porch, went into the bedroom he and Momma shared, and came out within a few minutes. The flat, misshapen old duffel now bulged with things inside it. It was clear he had packed as if he were going on a trip. He stopped and looked over at me for the first time.

"I've got to go," he said.

I am not sure how I knew it, but the look on his face told me he was leaving, and he would not be coming back. He headed down the hall toward the front door. I had to stop him! I grabbed ahold of his trouser leg and wrapped myself around him. I was so confused. If I had done something wrong, all he had to do was tell me, and I would have told him I was sorry. I had to stop him, I had to find out, and I did not want my father to go away.

"Amy, let go."

"Don't go." I began to cry.

I am not sure if he ever realized he had walked the entire length of the hall to the door with me clinging to him, but he had. At the front door, he grabbed my arms, loosening my grip on him. He sat me in the middle of the hall, and I watched as he disappeared through the door, which shut with a soft thud. My father was gone. The only thing I did not know was why. I sat there alone. It was a very long time before I even moved from the spot. Shadows had begun to form along the walls, which told me the sun was going down. I got up and walked to my room. Momma finally came home with my younger sisters with her. She bathed and dressed them and put them to bed.

From that point on, I witnessed Momma's life turn upside down. She had three young daughters to feed and clothe, a land payment, babysitters, and utilities to contend with. My father, I would come to discover later, had never been prompt with child support checks. She took a second job, and we scarcely saw her at all. A neighbor came and spent the night with us girls when Momma would work midnight shift at a local hospital at the switchboard.

After the divorce, we navigated through the splitting of summer vacations and holidays for the first few years. My father had remarried. I noticed how much of a challenge this had become, not only for my sister Beth and myself, but for the adults as well. Having to maintain a connection between all of us had become difficult and confusing. Over time, the visits, phone calls, letters, and birthday cards all slowed and then stopped altogether. I began to seek meaning in those absences and finally came to what I felt was the truth: my father no longer loved us and no longer cared. It made it easier to drift away from him. That estrangement would last for nearly a decade.

My father remained somewhat of a stranger to me the remainder of his life. We did reconcile, and he had seen his grandchildren, our daughters, as they grew up. Through the years, we had managed to visit one another as frequently as we could. I recalled one visit I had had with him just a few years before he died; he had spoken of his own parents' divorce nearly half a century earlier. At some point in time, my father had had to leave his mother and older sisters in the Midwest and travel to California, where he lived with his father, my grandfather. His father had begun a new life, with a new wife and family. He told me he often had felt as if he did not belong, out of place with them all, and very much alone. I sat and listened to him talk. He had known great pain in his young life.

The visit to the big house had brought clarity to me, and closure. God had arranged the invitation to the big house that night and had made sure I had been there. He had planned it years earlier, after what had transpired between my parents, and between my father and myself, the day he left. He had somehow made a way for the adult me to navigate through the maze of fear and pain and blame following my parents' divorce. Our lives had not been easy at the start, but along our path, He had provided me with something else—a stepdad, who became the father I was in desperate need of. God had known that every little girl needed a father. The love and stability that came to me as a result had given me the strength and ability to reach out to my natural father and rebuild a relationship with him. God had worked all things to good. I believe that Momma left that house in peace, at last.

Momma and I would never go back to the big house again.

We no longer needed to.

11

The Right Stuff

A man either had it or he didn't! There was no such
thing as having most of it.[1]

"He ought to be about your age now, right? Chuck Yeager?" I asked.

"Oh no," Dad corrected me. "He's an old guy."

We were standing beneath Glamorous Glynnis, the plane
that had broken the sound barrier over the desert in California at
Edwards Air Force Base. We were at the National Air and Space
Museum in Washington, DC. Dad, of course, loved the place. It
wasn't long after entering that we found ourselves standing under
and staring up at the bright-orange, very small plane. Dad was
mesmerized. He reached for it unconsciously, but it was just out of
arm's reach. I can still see his face fully in my mind to this day. As I
investigated his face, I had a strange feeling as if I were suddenly the
parent of an overactive little boy who was edging toward something
marked "Do not touch." I expected him to climb the rail and grab
the plane. Specifically, he seemed to be reaching for the hatch door.
My stepfather Don was barely five feet, eight inches tall. But he
suddenly seemed much taller as he stood there beneath the very first
rocket plane, painted international orange and named for the wife
of its test pilot, Chuck Yeager.

"Orange?" I screwed up my face. It was quite gaudy.

"Never mind that!" he countered quickly. His eyes did not leave the plane as he spoke. "It's what Yeager did with this plane, not the color it was!"

I smiled as I continued to watch him eye every single inch of the plane. Even then, I do not think Dad had ever taken the time to reflect on his own life, the things he had done. He simply did not think that way. His focus had always been on his commitment to his family, his work, everyday things. I knew how fortunate I had been to have a dad like that.

He came to us when I was not quite eleven, bouncing down the rutted red rock road that no one, absolutely no one, came down by accident. It led to the home I shared with Momma and my two sisters. His car was old and black, and that's all I can tell you about it. There are people who can tell the make of a car by the hubcaps, the style of the headlights, or the grille. Not me. All I knew was we were forever finding springs and bolts and various bits of it strewn along the road after his visits. It was my thought that one day the thing would fall apart altogether around him as he headed down the hill toward our house and leave him sitting on the dirt road with whatever happened to be left of the car sitting in piles all around him.

He had made a difference in our lives from the beginning. First off, Momma seemed to like him and look forward to his weekly visits. But to us girls, it was having someone around that could fix a leaky sink or tighten a doorknob. A few years later, they were married. It took some time, but somewhere during those early years, Don ceased being my momma's husband and became my dad. I hadn't thought of it then, but it had to be difficult, entering an environment of all females. I had no brothers, but that didn't seem to bother Dad. All of us girls had chores to do, especially helping to maintain the Christmas tree farm on our property.

To Dad, I wasn't a son or a daughter; he just loved to talk with me, regaling me with stories of his childhood on the wide, empty plains of Kansas at the farm where he had grown up. He was always available to talk. Mostly, I just listened.

Close to my senior year of high school, my parents received a form letter from the school. No, it wasn't a problem, just an interview with the guidance counselor that he did with all students who would be graduating that spring. Dad took time off work to go with me.

We both sat there, scrunched into two small chairs facing Mr. Flatt's desk. He suddenly popped up behind a stack of manila folders and books. He was holding a file in his hand. My name was on it. He shook my father's hand and began perusing my slender folder in a casual manner.

"You know, Amy doesn't type very well. That's a problem. Her math skills are marginal. No hard sciences, either." He paused for a time and then sighed.

"Amy doesn't seem to have any behavioral problems; in fact, she is very quiet and doesn't talk much." He was talking about me as if I wasn't even in the room. But it was about that time that he looked directly at me. Then he looked over at Dad.

"I think," Mr. Flatt began again, "she could possibly do some secretarial work if it didn't involve too much typing. Or perhaps teaching, though I don't see where she has even applied for any colleges," he added as he flipped through a few pages of my file. Then he closed it and added it to one of the tall piles of files on his desk.

"You know, she might just marry, not mess with any of that. That would be a good option."

I glanced over at Dad. His face was red. He leaned forward, staring at the guidance counselor for quite a long time; then he reached up and began scratching the back of his head. A very, very bad sign. It was Dad's signature move; he did this when he was extremely irritated at someone or something. I looked back at Mr. Flatt. He was in trouble, and he didn't even know it.

My dad slowly stood and reached for me. He pulled me up till I was standing beside him. Then, in a quiet, measured voice, Dad spoke: "Apparently, you don't know my daughter very well."

We left Mr. Flatt sitting there, his mouth ajar amidst all his little towers of files.

"Had you ever been to his office before?" Dad asked as we walked briskly to the parking lot.

"No," I said.

"You mean to say that in the four years you were there, he never called you into his office to just talk to you about what you wanted to do after high school?"

"No." In fact, that was the first time I had ever met him and the very first time he had ever called me by name. I knew others who had gone in and out of his office during my high school years. My grades were average. Attention was paid in those days to those who excelled in math and sciences. I excelled at none of those.

Dad stopped at the stop sign near the main road. He looked over at me.

"Now, you don't believe any of what he said in there, do you?" His voice was filled with incredulity.

I shook my head.

In years to come, my parents would feel a great deal of pride and not disbelief when I became a nurse. As for me, I carry within me a personal sense of accomplishment knowing I type well over a hundred words a minute on my computer. Listening to the counselor that day might have left me disheartened. Mr. Flatt's uninformed opinions about my life, my academics, and my prospects seemed unimportant and inconsequential at that exact moment. My dad believed in me. That was what mattered.

In late 1996, when he and Momma were visiting us, he did not feel well and had to go in for a chest x-ray. The results were not good, and he was advised to go home at once and consult his doctor. The following spring, he would die, following a hard-fought battle with metastatic lung cancer. I have thought of all the many conversations we had over the years. But my thoughts go back to the last one. It was the night before he died. I had called to speak with him.

"Oh, Amy," Momma said softly. "He won't understand you. He won't hardly respond to anything anymore." But I told her to put the phone to his ear just the same. She did.

"Dad, I know you don't feel well, but I have to tell you something," I began, hardly knowing where to begin. "I know we weren't your children, and you didn't have to take us on, but you did. You were so brave! I am so grateful for you. Thank you, Dad. You've been a good dad. I love you." My words were brief. I wasn't sure he even heard them, much less understood them. But I had to tell him. I had to.

"What did you say?" Momma was back on the phone. "He's crying." So was I.

I was honored to eulogize Dad at his funeral. He was buried in the little farming community he had grown up in out on the Kansas prairie, with full military honors. Dad had served in the navy during World War 2.

A few weeks after our return home from the funeral, a letter arrived, addressed to me. It was from a distant cousin who had attended Dad's funeral.

> Amy, I knew Don only as a young teenager during the summer when I worked for our uncles early in World War 2. I hardly saw your dad for forty years, and the few times I did I was cordial, but not anxious to spend time trying to know him better. Your stories about him made me realize how shallow a person can be and sorry I hadn't the maturity to understand the man you described.

I told several stories about Dad during my eulogy; one had been about the guidance counselor I had in high school. I found myself smiling. I continued to read the cousin's letter, and my eye caught on his last few sentences: "I have a stepdaughter," he continued, "whom I acquired at about the same age you described, and if God permits me to look down at my funeral one day and hear her say half of what you said about your dad I'll consider myself a success."

I thought of Dad's hero, Chuck Yeager. Dad didn't have a college degree. Neither did Chuck Yeager. The legacy Yeager left was in the testing of many prototype planes, putting them through their paces, discovering what they were made of. And Dad? His legacy to me was just as profound. He had been a gift to a young girl. A dad who could be depended upon, who would remain faithful to my momma for as long as he lived. Through the years, Dad showed me what I believe to be true to this day: what we become is a result of what our fathers teach us. It is not found in lecturing with longwinded cautionary tales. It is not in bold, worldly accomplishment. No—it happens in those moments, large and small, orchestrated by God, when they are not even aware they are teaching us anything at all. My life continues to be filled with memories of those.

My hero, my staunch defender, my protector, my friend.

My dad had the right stuff.

12

Broken

> Not until we have passed through the furnace are
> we made to know how much dross there is in our
> composition.[1]

As we entered Tim and Katie's* house, there were over a dozen couples on sofas, chairs, and benches. Katie's eyes widened as she looked at me; Tim went to the garage and set up two folding chairs for us. They had been calling us for weeks, encouraging us to meet with a group they had gotten together who wanted to share questions and concerns.

"It isn't just us!" Katie whispered to me.

Leah appeared from the kitchen, a piece of paper clutched tightly in her hand. She greeted us quietly, and together we stood staring out at the people that crowded the living room that day. Two couples we did not recognize were present. They had attended the fellowship but had left three years earlier. We knew the rest. There were musicians, writers, artists in all mediums, sound board operators, administrators, office personnel, intercessors. These were the faithful—in their presence, in their tithe, in their efforts and energies. It was not a megachurch, but it had been a busy one, seemingly filled with life and purpose. But something had changed. The place where we had all felt safe and the place where we had felt called to serve God with our gifts had changed. Perhaps the system had been in place that whole time, but we had simply been too busy to have noticed. We felt like victims but didn't know why.

Church splits were becoming common in the country. Some churches had never recovered, closing their doors after decades and not reopening. Other start-up churches we had seen had grown too quickly, without proper guidance and prayer. Their focus, limited to a single aspect of church life, such as worship, fellowship, or missions, was leaving parking lots filled with sheep who went the door only to find no one at home, even though the doors were still open. The area where we lived at the time had a church on very nearly every corner. But on any given Sunday, there might have been a half dozen cars at many of them. I wondered why.

Leah gathered everyone's attention.

"I have something to read, and I want you to just listen," she said quietly. "I hope it can start a discussion, so we can understand what we have been through."

Everyone seemed to nod in unison. For thirty minutes, she read from a prepared list from our search of the internet and in books we had never thought existed, or should have existed. Her words were objective and void of emotion as she read. What she read had no mercy or regard for those who were listening. The faces I observed looked as if someone were reading a very personal and private letter aloud about them to the entire room. I had no doubt some of them felt violated. As Leah finished speaking, they seemed to do what animals do when sensing a predator nearby: they froze in place, not breathing.

A slow, low hum of conversation began. It started with a group sitting on the sofa; then it spread throughout the room. Gradually, most of the group stood, and some wandered into the kitchen, reaching for mugs, pouring coffee, hoping to do something normal. Most had heard their own, personal experience recited from what Leah had read aloud.

We hadn't attended there long and had not forged the bonds

that many of those in the kitchen had. Yet all of us shared stories of the common response toward us by those who had remained in the fellowship. Most of the people we would encounter would barely acknowledge us when we met them in the grocery store or on the street. If we did manage to engage them, they would respond to us with shallow conversation and cold smiles of distrust. These were the people I was thinking of at that moment, still in their places under the control of the leaders. I use that word because It is difficult for me, even to this day, to refer to the place as a church, and even more difficult to think of the leader as a pastor. No one sitting in the room that day wanted to confess that we had belonged to a group that fit the exact description of a cult. And certainly, none of us wanted to confess we had been victims of spiritual abuse.

We would never all meet again as we had the day, though several smaller groups were formed out of that first, large one. We would get together, talk, pray, and seek updates on each other's well-being. News would come to us individually of some finding a new church home, some still searching for the perfect church. For my family, three months had passed before we found a new church home. Some couples and individuals had moved out of town, one couple had divorced, and a few had refused to return to church of any sort agai. Many had cited the list read that day as a motivator to move along, move past the abuse they felt and into freedom. One lady kept in contact with me. Her name was Sue.

Sue and I, along with half a dozen other ladies, had formed a small group. It seemed important to have those people who had shared the experience close to us and share our grief. Yes, grief. We had suffered a loss. It would keep us honest in what we had been through. No one else would know our story but those who had been there and often had witnessed it firsthand. We met at one another's homes, usually once a week. For a time, we managed to downgrade our own personal experiences. We had been keenly aware that we had heard both similar and worse stories from those who had shared at that first meeting at Tim and Katie's home. We began by looking into the mirror of the Word. As we studied, light began to filter into our individual situations. Meeting together began to feel like healing itself as we shared our new freedoms and insights within the safety we felt with one another. In time, we came to the place where we were able to share our discoveries and our personal experiences with each other in depth.

A leader had told Sue, after she had revealed several long-forgiven sins during an inner healing class, that she did not seem repentant enough, and that he doubted she had been forgiven at all. He had then told her that she could not be used by God. Not in her state. Even after time had passed and some healing had come, it was difficult for her to speak about any of it.

It would be many weeks later, as we delved into a few books and articles on spiritual abuse, that we would make a discovery that caught us totally off guard: each of us had a hook, if you will—a flaw, such as shame, fear, pride, unforgiveness, ignorance of the Word of God, some sort of stronghold in our lives that had allowed the abuser to latch onto us. Through those strongholds in our hearts and minds, we had inadvertently enabled our own abusers to control and manipulate us. It was no easy matter not to reject the notion outright that we had played a part in our own spiritual abuse. But in most of our cases, it had been true. Had we been poor stewards? When you are so busy "serving," you have little time to see what is going on around you spiritually in other areas. That, I believe, had been a big problem, and the first tool used against us all. We had been hand-selected for that very reason.

In my own private thoughts, I did not know which had been worse: being deceived or playing a part in my own deceit. For myself, it was the matter of not wanting to fail God in pursuit of my ministry within the church—a works mentality. For Sue, it had been the shame of a former sin, forgiven long ago. It had revealed to her the doubts she had about her forgiveness, had created in her a lack of trust in any leadership within the church, and had cued the shame buried deep in her heart. I had a very similar experience. The fact that each of us had believed blindly in the leader, because he was in authority, had revealed to each of us that we had no idea what the true Biblical interpretation of authority within God's church was.

One of the women in our group confessed she had tried to speak with the leader about a matter, only to be told she lacked spirituality, and had been placed immediately into an inner healing class so the leadership could help them root out the reasons for her bad attitudes. This information would later be exploited by the leader to privately shame her. For her, remaining in the fellowship was not an option, so she left, dragging her weary and tattered heart and soul with her.

My family's decision had come after a month of deliberation. Though our decisions and departing would vary, each of us in the group knew what the fallout would be. We had heard it before, when other couples or families or individuals had simply vanished from the fellowship. Leadership, and those who were close to their inner circle, never spoke of them again. Occasionally comments would be made to quell the gossip within the fellowship. Those who had gone, leadership stated, were "no longer part of the team"; they "did not have the mission in their hearts." Shocking to many of us when we heard them were the pronouncements of what we thought sounded like curses coming from the leader directed at those who had left the fellowship: "Bad things happen to those who leave. They get sick; their finances are ruined. You don't want that to happen to you!"

Early on, we discussed the damage the fellowship had done to us and was continuing to do to those who remained in the fellowship. One grieved the loss of ministry opportunity, whining about not being used by God anymore. Another felt God had abandoned them totally. The conversations around the room were revealing. Would we recognize them as our difficulties?

"You know," Sue commented during a meeting one evening. "This stuff makes me wonder if it's possible to ever trust a pastor again." The question was not in her voice. It was in her eyes.

"We tried going to another church last Sunday. Jim refused

to get out of the car, so we sat in the parking lot. After about five minutes, we just drove away."

In time, even our smaller group of survivors disbanded. I was later to hear that Sue and Jim had found a new church home. They had relocated to be closer to their grown children, several states away. The true gift for us all was when we realized that the experience had revealed chinks in our armor, exposing roots of our very beliefs. We have gone on to serve the Lord with gladness, unafraid. Some in the group have remained unchanged, broken, and in need of mending. That is something that only God can do. It was during those meetings that I began to understand that this broken church experience had been a gift. Grace had brought us to that place for a season, and that same grace had brought us out again safely and into a wide and level place. Truth was there. And light. For most of us, change came. And peace.

13

Gone

I stared blankly at the man before me. There had been only one word I had heard clearly throughout his entire very loud outburst.

"Gone!"

The son of one of my patients on the second floor was angry about something; I just did not know what.

"Gone?" I parroted. I regretted it at once, but it was too late. Mr. Henley's eyes narrowed on me.

"Yes, gone!" His voice had tempered somewhat, perhaps because he finally realized he was shouting. "There were two of them, and now they are gone. I want to know what you are going to do about it."

It took a few more moments to ascertain that the two he was speaking of were nightgowns. Specifically, nightgowns that belonged to his mother. Most residents had their laundry done within the facility. But there were some families that preferred to pick up their loved ones' laundry. More than likely, his mother's nightclothes had found their way into a laundry hamper and then into the facility laundry room. He wanted them found. Now.

I assured him I would investigate it and left the nursing station, scanning the hallway for hampers. *Too bad Mary wasn't here today,* I recall thinking at that moment. She would have known right where those nightgowns had gone to. The elderly Mrs. Henley was one of

Mary's regular patients. I summoned the nursing assistant assigned to the hall that night to accompany me on the search.

"That man is really mad, Miss Amy." Sallie, the nursing assistant, ran alongside me, trying to keep up.

"Do you know where to start looking?" I asked. Sallie shook her head.

"Not a clue. Mary might know. I could call her at home."

I dismissed the notion at once. Mary had only one night off that week, and I wasn't about to disturb her.

"It isn't like she needs those gowns," Sallie protested as we came around a corner into the small laundry sorting area. "She's got an entire dresser full!"

"Nonetheless, they are her gowns, and we need to find them," I finished, and separated myself from Sallie's truthful prattling. "So please keep your eyes open for them."

I proceeded down the next hall and had not gone far before I heard my name over the intercom. *Well, that was quick,* I reasoned. *Sallie must have found those gowns.* But as I listened, I was being summoned to the director's office. *Oh no.* Mr. Henley had gone to the office without giving us as chance to find those gowns! I slipped down a stairway and opened the door to the first floor. Mrs. Cook, the director, was sitting in her office, engrossed in a phone call. The door was open, and she waved me in through her open door.

"You need to get in here," she said as she pointed to an empty chair in front of her desk and hung the phone up. "Shut that," she said curtly as she pointed to the door. I did. I was about to begin a protest about the missing nightgowns when she spoke.

"I don't know how to tell you this, so I guess I have to just come out with it. I need to let you know so you can adjust the schedules. Mary is dead. She committed suicide last night. Her husband found her, and—well, it was a mess. Anyway, she's gone."

Gone.

I sat in stunned silence for a while. Then a silent tidal wave of rage, fear, betrayal, and sadness, all in equal measure, swept over me all at once. Then I spoke the first thing that came into my mind.

"That can't be right. I just worked with her yesterday."

Mrs. Cook looked up at me with something like compassion.

"Well, that was yesterday, Amy. She's gone."

In my mind, I ticked off the signs to watch for: the verbal cues, the body language, the physical symptoms of a depressive episode. I had seen none of these in Mary. People who are going to kill themselves will usually speak of it, and perhaps look for a way to make it happen. If she had said any of those things in my presence, I would have recalled them, been alert. No—Mary Herndon did not fit the profile of a suicide risk in any way.

"Well, why?" was all I could manage. Mrs. Cook adjusted her glasses and looked up from a stack of papers.

"Nobody really knows things like that, do they? At least, her daughter didn't say anything about it this morning when she called."

I found my way back to the nursing station upstairs. I heard the break room down the hall alive with chattering voices. These, as far as I knew, were Mary's closest coworkers—her friends for many years. I didn't know how I was going to tell them. I heard a stirring behind me in the hall and looked up to see Glenna, Mary's daughter, coming toward me. Her eyes were red, and it took some time for her to speak. I quickly led her away from the noisy hallway and into a smaller, more private room off the nursing station. My own voice was suddenly unfamiliar to me as I attempted to express my profound sorrow at her loss. The words seemed hollow. I felt lost in the despair I saw in Glenna's face.

"I don't know how to ask this." She straightened herself up and took a seat on the sofa next to me. Her voice sounded thin. "I was just wondering if you could tell me—what sort of day did Mom have yesterday?"

Yesterday? Did she think something had happened at work? I retraced the entire shift the evening before in my mind. I could think of nothing out of the ordinary. It had been a normal evening.

I listened as Glenna, filled with guilt, was attempting to piece her mother's life back together, to find a way to understand. Her feelings of guilt and shame were evident. Worse, she said she might have been able to have stopped it, if only she had seen the signs. When she left the hall, I realized I could not help Glenna with the answers to the questions she was so desperately seeking.

Before she left, I took time with Glenna to tell her what I knew of her mother. She did her work efficiently, created no trouble, and never took long breaks. She never complained. In a business where call-ins were frequent and working shorthanded was a daily affair, Mary was faithful to show up for her shifts early and often stayed late. I shared remembrances of her soothing voice as she reassured a confused patient. Mary always seemed to have the ability to read the moods of her patients and quell their fears and concerns. What I did not tell Glenna was that Mary and I had walked out the of building the night before together. We had been less than two feet apart from each other, and we had not spoken at all.

I went home, heartsick and confused. My husband sat in his easy chair, waiting up for me. I wanted to tell him what had happened, but I had trouble forming the words. Finally, the words came.

"One of my aides killed herself last night." The words felt hard as they fell from my mouth.

My husband dropped his magazine to his lap and stared as I relayed the story Glenna had told me that evening. My mind could not forget Glenna's visit, her words, her horrible grief, nor her questions to me.

That night, I fell into a restless sleep, awakened from time to time by faces in my dreams. Faces of people I knew. Family members, coworkers, patients I had cared for. I saw Mary, too. As I looked at them, I had to admit to myself that many of them were not well known to me. Not quite strangers, but—what did I really know about any of them? Like Glenna, I had taken on the unrealistic feelings of guilt and shame over Mary's death, as if I could have prevented it somehow. But none of us had seen it coming. To be honest, I was haunted by Mary's death.

In the weeks and months to come, in my conversations with Glenna and with Mary's coworkers, I discovered very little. There had been no changes at home, no painful events going on, no sudden changes. Life was just, as Glenna had put it through tears that day, normal. Mary had not been ill, nor was there a history of any sort of mental disorders in her family. Knowing all that, I then found myself frustrated and angry with Mary. I wished she would come back and explain herself to all those who cared about her. But my anger brought only silence. It was in that silence that I finally began to learn a difficult lesson about Mary's death.

It began right in the middle of my trying to understand it all; I walked down the halls at work, through the mall, and down the tiny aisles of the grocery store—there were the trite exchanges people made with each other that I really had not paid much attention to before. But I was paying attention now. I would hear the occasional "How are you?" while the person who had asked it continued walking past, not bothering to listen to the reply. People did it again and again. How often had I done that without even a backward glance? I found myself wanting more because of Mary's death. I did not want to miss another opportunity to connect with another, if that connection was one that would matter to the other person's life.

Not long ago, I saw a sampler stitched in a delicate cross stitch hanging on a wall at an antique store. It said:

Bless our home, Father.
That we may cherish the bread before there is none,
Discover each other before we leave,
And enjoy each other for what we are while we have time.

When I saw it, I thought how nice it would look on my wall. Later that week, I returned to the place where I had seen it, intent on purchasing it. It had been sold. I have thought of those few words a great deal, but to have the meaning of them in my heart—that is something worth striving for always.

I still miss Mary.

(If you are struggling with thoughts of suicide, please reach out to your pastor, your doctor, a friend, or the twenty-four-hour National Suicide Prevention Hotline at 1-800-273-8255 (TALK) in the US. For hotlines outside the United States, go to suicide.org.)

14

Enough

And God is able to bless you abundantly, so that in all things at all times, having all that you need, you will abound in every good work.

—2 Corinthians 9:8 (NIV)

"I'm doing all I can—I just don't know if it is enough."

The memory of those words presented itself to me one morning as I stood in the laundry room, preparing to do a few loads before lunch time. The words I recalled that morning we not mine; they had been Momma's. And though I hadn't spoken them out loud, I had certainly thought them in the years since Momma had come to live with Galen and myself.

I suppose there is a time in everyone's life when we question our abilities to accomplish a task. Our prayers and our thoughts, however, seem only to confirm a hidden fear that we just may not be up to the challenge ahead of us. I was doing my best to be sensible, rational, and positive. But it wasn't until God specifically laid the task before me, and assured me that it was mine, that I really began to doubt. I had cared for scores of people during my career as a geriatric nurse. But none of them was my momma.

It had been Momma that had said those words to me decades

ago. Then, as well as when I had recollected them in my laundry room that morning, they had taken my surprise. She said them as we were about to leave after a visit one summer. We had piled our suitcases in the car and had settled down in our seats when she leaned though the window and whispered them to me. There had been no time to respond, no time to process what she had said. There was something in her voice I did not recognize that day that had cemented the words into my memory. Her words were fearful, uncertain. But that day in the laundry room, I realized I recognized that voice. I stood there in the laundry room, remembering her words, and I understood them completely.

Momma had always been the most efficient, even-tempered person I had ever known. Those words, spoken so long ago, made me realize that Momma had once felt the way I was now feeling. It had been a confusing time for her back then. She had been working full time, was a wife and a mother, and was also caring for her own mother, my grandma Lizzie.

For as long as I can recall, we always had one relative or another living with us for extended periods of time. Lizzie, my momma's momma, was a regular houseguest. There came a time when she had come to live with my parents on a permanent basis. That summer, on one of our visits to the coast, I noticed the changes in Lizzie. She was a diabetic prone to obesity, and her condition had deteriorated. The table that sat beside her chair had once been covered in colorful skeins of yarn and crochet hooks. Now it was dotted with bottles of medication. I also noted a new grouping of medication bottles lining the windowsill in the kitchen. Those belonged to Momma.

Momma arranged for nurses to come for visits while she was at work. They helped Lizzie bathe, checked her medication, blood sugar, and blood pressure, and dressed her wounds that never seemed to heal properly. Momma never mentioned the heavy load it had placed on her emotionally and physically until just before we were about to leave.

It was not long after our visit that Lizzie had to be admitted to the hospital for some routine tests. A breast cancer survivor, she was now discovered to have metastatic bone cancer. They transferred her directly from her hospital room to a sunny, small room at a nearby nursing home. Momma was no longer able to care for her, as Lizzie would need twenty-four-hour care. Momma continued her vigil. She would go daily after work and remain in the nursing home to feed Lizzie her dinner and then tuck her into bed each night with the promise that she would be there the next day for a visit. One day, within an hour of Momma's visit, Lizzie slipped from her cancer-ravaged body and died quietly in her sleep.

On one of my many lengthy trips to California to tend to Momma after her heart surgery, I was cleaning her office. I came across a notebook that had fallen behind her desk. It was filled with notes she had kept when she had attended an evangelism class at her church. I began to read: "I had been in several churches in different states during my life, still thinking I was a Christian. But I didn't really have a relationship God until April 27, 1998. On that day I lost my husband, Don, to lung cancer," she had written.

> When Don died, I had many discussions with a pastor who had become a family friend. I had recently moved from my house in the country that I shared with Don and into a senior citizen's trailer park. I wasn't going to church at all. The pastor began to question me about my own faith. I told him I felt I was a pretty good person. But I came to understand that wasn't enough. And I was to discover that God had an ongoing purpose for my life, and the only way I could experience it was to accept Jesus into my heart. I did that on December 20, 1998, and was then baptized. Walking with Him is not always easy, but I do know that by going to church, praying, reading His Word, and listening for the Holy Spirit's prompting, I will get through!

As I continued to read the pages in her notebook, I discovered page after page that had documented a profound transformation in Momma. Momma has always been a self-described homebody, and rather shy. I was surprised as I read about the challenge her pastor issued to the entire congregation to step out of their comfort zones to participate in an outreach ministry in their community. This single event would stretch Momma in ways she had never experienced in her new walk with God. In this outreach, she would learn to share her testimony, her faith, and experiences of life with others—a tall order for a quiet, rather reserved woman like Momma. But she began to meet with the other parishioners every Monday evening for seven weeks of training. In time, they went out to various parts of the town to visit with members of the community.

"I have to learn to do this, but I am really scared," she penned. "We have all gone out a few times, and I have actually prayed that wherever we are sent that they would *all* be Christians, so I won't have to share at all! This is really hard for me to do."

And then September 11, 2001, happened.

> 9/11 made me realize that I needed to go over to Bakersfield and see my sister, Christine. So, I just got real brave, drove to Bakersfield, and when we had spent some time together, I said to her, "Chris, if you should die tonight are you sure you would go to heaven?" She said she wasn't sure, so there was my chance and I didn't waste any time. On September 13, 2001, I led my sister to the Lord. She was 77 years old. What a joy I felt and what a comfort to know that we will be together in heaven.

That single experience at her church had been the start of a deeper understanding of the power of the message of the gospel of Christ for her. It seemed to charge her with an urgency and a purpose. She soon shed her fears and other concerns. Momma's faith became evident in every area of her life as she came to understand God and His provision through many rough patches in her life, as well as in the many joys. Feeding and clothing the poor, inviting others to church, being part of hosting church meetings and Bible studies brought her a sense of immense fulfillment and true purpose. Her favorite work was working for God, wherever He placed her.

Momma headed up the hospitality committee at church, where she served behind the scenes at many dinners, within the church and during outreach ministries. She served on the pastoral search committee and was on the business committee. She was treasurer of her Sunday school class and would sit alone after class ended, counting and logging the offering. I know this because I sat with her during those times in her later years when she had begun to have difficulty staying on task.

"Can you just check this amount?" she would ask me each Sunday when I was with her. "One more time—I just want to be sure."

There came a time when the streets she had known and driven for fifty years had become frighteningly unfamiliar to her. She willingly gave up the keys to her car. A more daunting and difficult task was having to give up her church work. But she eventually resigned all her positions. It became clear that Momma couldn't be alone at home anymore. She would often go out into the yard and water flowers in the middle of the night or wander through the house at three a.m., thinking it was morning. One morning, she woke up and could no longer figure out how to make a pot of coffee or use her phone. During the days I was with her, I would organize and pay her bills, tend to her legal issues, take her to doctor's appointments, and make sure her home was safe for her to wander about in. We would take long drives, watch sunsets at the beach, grocery shop together, and watch favorite television programs when they were on. We also went to church several times a week. Being able to go to church with Momma was an absolute anchor for me. With each new difficulty, a word would come from the pulpit that I felt was just for me or that related in some way to a situation I was finding myself in with Momma. My sister, Beth, stepped up, and I trained her as best I could so she could take charge when I wasn't there. We were a great team. For over five years, I would travel back and forth from the Midwest to California, staying weeks to months with Momma at a time in her little trailer.

At some point, Momma finally made the decision to come and live with Galen and myself. When she came to live with us, it was a source of great relief and joy to our family. She made a new home with us, and we were all adjusting to our new lives together. Galen had not yet retired, and we were basically empty nesters, so I had Momma all to myself much of the time. I enjoyed these times, after living away from her for so long. Momma's memories became jumbled at times, but the times of her childhood flowed easily from her. During those days, she shared stories of her four brothers and one sister, and Lizzie. Stories of working in the fields in Oklahoma, tales of dust storms, shoeless summers, and cold winters.

"Everyone was in the same fix," she would always tell me. "No one had much, but we didn't know it, so it was fine. We always had good food and each other."

Momma had gone to a one-room schoolhouse in Manitou, Oklahoma. During the winter months, she had to wrap her feet in burlap to make the trip to Holden School. It was several miles from their home, and they had no horse or mule. Yes—she did walk two miles to school! Even in the snow. She recalled the name of a teacher who had taught her, a Miss Pinson.

"In the spring, we walked through the pasture with cows in it. You know, sometimes there were bulls in there. I wasn't afraid because the boys were around. It was nice to have big brothers."

They moved as a family to California in 1941, where they had all found work in the fields, pulling cotton or digging potatoes or onions. Unlike many of the Okies, they had a house awaiting them in Bakersfield. Momma had been the first person in her family to finish high school.

"When Howard went to war, I watched him go. I was twelve years old," she said quietly one day as we were watching a program about Pearl Harbor. "When he came home, he came home in in taxi! None of us had ever ridden in one before. Taxis were for rich people, you know. But there it was, right in front of the house. And he walked to do the door and he said to me, 'Hi, sis!' My brother was home."

One day, while she was reminiscing, her eyes got watery.

"Do you want to go with me?" she asked.

"Where, Momma?" I asked.

"To see Mom, at her house." Lizzie had been gone nearly thirty years. Then her eyes changed. She realized her mistake. "Oh, she's gone, isn't she?"

I nodded.

"You have told me that before, and I forgot." She frowned at her inability to recall. "How many times will you have to tell me that?"

"As long as you need it, Momma."

In truth, Momma was the last of her family. Her four brothers, a sister, and both parents were gone. Even so, I would often hear her as she rehearsed their names and wondered where each of them lived and what they were doing. She would tell me later that she had always known they were gone; she just liked to talk about them.

A year passed, and then another, and I began to sense a change in myself. I was not just physically exhausted, but spiritually exhausted as well. It had been many months since Momma had felt well enough to go to church. I had nearly always stayed home with her. I brought her to our home, already exhausted mentally and physically from the frequent travels I had made to and from California, away from family and friends for months at a time. Now, in my present situation, I felt just as unavailable as I had been when I had been traveling.

Momma went through a period of months where her mini strokes seemed to have stopped. But then she would have one or two in rapid cadence. She never recalled having the mini strokes, for which I was quite grateful. But the effects of previous strokes had taken a toll on her. She never came back to full strength. She began spending less time talking and more time paying attention to the birds at the birdfeeder outside the window near her chair.

One mid-November morning, while I was preparing her breakfast, I glanced at her open doorway. If I hadn't looked that way, I might have missed it. I saw a glow coming softly from her room, and I stuck my head in quietly in time to observe the morning sunlight settle on her bed. I stopped for time and marveled at it and realized I had not witnessed a sunrise in a long time. Momma's face was bathed in the soft glow coming from her window. I quietly thanked God for it.

"I think I know why I have lived so long," she said that morning at breakfast. I stared at her. "It's because I ate cornbread, beans, and fried potatoes. And we had a big garden and we ate everything out of that! I really do think that's the reason. I really do."

I could not argue with that. Her ability to make complete sentences had been rare over the past weeks. Now she had made several complete sentences in a row. I quietly thanked God for that, as well.

Momma died on December 25th of that year. Her final stroke had been a massive one. We had decided to celebrate Christmas, but my heart was not at all in it. It was a quiet celebration of Momma's life. The thing was, it had been Momma's favorite holiday, and it seemed a shame not to honor the day. Our family rallied together, and we prepared the food and set the table. We opened our gifts; then we ate and thanked God for His incredible gift of Jesus.

On the day we buried Momma, it was icy and cold. She was buried next to my stepdad in the little Kansas farming community that he had been raised in. I felt ill-prepared for the event and had wanted to do it properly. But the weather had made it impossible. I found a small florist shop on the way to the cemetery and asked what they might have on hand. Out that way, it was a bad time of year for fresh-cut flowers of any kind.

"Well, we have these. It is really all we have. I'm really very sorry," the clerk apologized. She pointed over to a large vase. Spilling out over the top of it were sprays of pink baby rosebuds. My eyes filled with tears at the sight of them. Those had been the flowers Momma had received from someone on the day I had been born. She had kept the delivery card and placed it in my baby book.

Pink baby rosebuds.

I nodded. "Those will do nicely."

Time passed, and I began to think of the normal things we had done together. Momma had loved to sit in her recliner and watch the birds swarm around the little birdfeeder outside the window. We took to watching nature shows on television, where we had seen giant box jellyfish and looked for Genghis Khan's tomb in Mongolia. At last count, we had visited each national park at least twice.

"Do you believe that thing is real?" She pointed to the television. We had been watching a documentary on Bigfoot.

"I don't know," I replied.

"I hope it's not." And that was all she had to say about that.

A large red bird flitted near the window and caught her eye for a moment. It perched on the feeder. A cardinal. All thoughts of Bigfoot had vanished.

"Chris?" she called. The last six months of her life, I had officially become her sister, who had died three years earlier. She had been Momma's best friend. I was honored. "Chris, what are you doing?"

"I'm here, Momma," I told her. "Just writing in my journal."

"Oh, that's good."

When I looked up again, she had fallen asleep.

God never gives us anything to do that He cannot enable us to accomplish. But, in our minds, we may say those very words Momma used that day so long ago. I had thought them, myself, while caring for her. *Is it enough?* If we depend upon His grace to sustain us, to bring us through, to allow us to accomplish what God assigns to us, I would say, He is more than enough.

Rest well, Momma.

15

The Unplowed Field

We must wait on God, long, meekly, in the wind
and wet, in the thunder and lightning, in the cold
and the dark. Wait, and he will come. He never
comes to those who do not wait. He does not go
on their road. When he comes, go with him, but
go slowly, fall a little behind; when he quickens his
pace, be sure of it before you quicken yours. But
when he slackens, slacken at once; and do not be
slow only, but silent, very silent, for he is God.[1]

It was the spring of 1983, and Galen had placed me on a tractor one
day at the farm. I was to pull a plow behind the tractor, and it was
my first time.

"Now, just look ahead. Put the right tire in the outer tire of
the round I just made," he began, pointing to the right tractor
tire. "Don't look back, because you are not going in that direction.
Concentrate on what's ahead, or you'll mess up your rows."

Everything in me wanted to look back to see if the row was neat
and tidy behind me; but I had to concentrate on the tire track ahead
of me, and on my right. The next round I made, I discovered I had
done a pretty good job at plowing that second row. He flagged me

down at the start of my third row and flung the cab of the tractor open for a bit.

"Remember, don't look back, because you're not going that way!" he yelled above the din of the old tractor.

As it would turn out, we would both need to heed that advice and keep our eyes on where we were going.

Late that summer, following harvest, Galen's father and business partner had grown too ill to be of help any longer. Since coming to live on the farm and taking over operations in 1978, some five years earlier, we had been completely hailed out two years in a row, our wheat crop flattened to the ground while we watched from the front porch, helpless. We suffered livestock loss from predation, once with the sheep herd and the other with a cow herd. Those barren years had been hard to bear for both of us, and costly financially. And there had always been the concern about his father's failing health. The partnership would be dissolved, and along with it the chance for Galen to continue farming. Galen had been born and raised in the small town. His grandfather had built the house we where we lived. Well-grounded and well-rooted elements abounded in his life. I was amazed at the solidness of it throughout the generations. Our daughter Sarah was the fifth generation of Robbinses to live at the family farm. Compared to Galen, I had been positively rootless. I had come from a broken home, moved dozens of times in my life, and attended many different schools. Galen had gone from kindergarten through high school with the same people, in the same town. Yet despite my upbringing and tenuous root system, my heart had become attached to the land, the farm, the life. I sensed a permanence and connection to it that I had never experienced before. We would sit out in the afternoon, following his dad's news, and listen to the meadowlarks call to us across the field and wonder why this would happen—and what would happen next.

The farm sale came that fall. The day of the sale, Galen said he almost felt relieved. All the equipment and miscellaneous items from the generations went up for auction. I watched from the window in our living room as the auctioneer worked the crowd. People would back up trucks and load boxes. The tractors and combine were loaded onto flatbed trucks and hauled away. The land would remain in the family; his parents would need the income from land rent to other farmers to meet their needs, due to his father's failing health. That was good, I reasoned. It was important that the land stay in the family. As I watched the tractor I had once pulled a plow behind being loaded onto a flatbed truck, I found myself remembering a walk Galen and I had had just after we moved out to the farm, five years earlier. We were newly married. We had walked up the lane to an expanse of land that looked a bit rough, scattered with thick grass and sage. It was pristine prairie.

"This ground has never been broken out. This is buffalo grass. See here." He kicked the ground and dislodged a large, thick clod of dirt, and grabbed it up. Then he handed it to me.

"This is sod. It's the stuff settlers used to build their houses when they came here. Nothing but grass has ever grown here."

I looked down at the clod thick with soil and realized it had always been there, long before Galen's family had even moved there. I looked out at the pasture, which seemed to roll and dip beneath the horizon ahead of us; the warmth of the wind seemed to cool somewhat. The day was nearly done. We stood there quietly and watched as the sun slid away. For me, it was a moment I would never forget. And I thought as we walked back to the house that evening, *This is my home, and I never have to leave here.* I had come there to a new home, as a new wife, in a new season of my own life. Five years had passed, and my life had consisted of my job as a nurse, writing, and now tending to our daughter, Sarah. Galen's life, the only life he had ever known, had been wrapped up in this piece of grass and dirt I had held in my hand.

We had known the difficulty of farming. In addition to weather events, there was a changing economy, and different farm policies. Farming had changed since the time his father had taken over the farm as a young man. We knew that we were not the only ones experiencing difficulties in holding onto our livelihoods. In our small town, the last of the railroad system had been pulled up and discarded; the farmers had opted to have their crops hauled by semis tino the terminal elevators in bigger towns. Smaller farms were dying, and none were being replaced. Big farmers gained more ground, consolidating into larger and larger areas; this made their production more efficient.

The farm sale lasted well into the afternoon, and as I continued to watch, I had no choice but to believe that another new season was coming. Change. I wasn't sure I wanted it. We both had jobs, in addition to the farm work. Now we would live on his contract pumping work with an oil company, a part-time position that turned into a full-time one shortly after our farm sale. I also worked part-time at the nursing home in town. We waited for a new door of promise to open to us, but none came. The life that seemed to have nourished Galen all his life, and had welcomed me, now seemed to be drying up from its roots. The farm, our church home, and the family it had provided us had been an anchor for us. But slowly we began to sense that we were out of place somehow, where we had once felt at home and at peace. We watched for several years as someone else farmed our land and harvested the crops that surrounded our farmhouse. God seemed silent to us as the months progressed. It was to the loudest silence I had ever heard in my life. In days, weeks, and months ahead, I read and reread Ecclesiastes, and the times and seasons for everything.[2] Our time for peace had not yet come. The oil field work played out not two years after Galen began working full-time, following the farm sale.

I thought of our daughter, Sarah, who was nearly six. She had grown up knowing only life at the farm, with its own seasons of planting, growth, harvest, and winter's rest. This new season would bring changes to her life. All our stories, our shared history with generations, the wide Kansas prairie, the hissing and waving of the wheat growing tall in the fields around the house that she and I would run through and get lost in. Playing in the clothesline, hiding in the wind-dried clothes in the backyard. The constant blowing of the wind and the quiet nights with a sky filled with stars overhead. All that would vanish from her eyes. Would she remember any of it? *So little time,* I thought. *So little time.* A new season was coming—for all three of us.

We had accepted a position working for a poultry farmer, which Galen had said was still working in agriculture—sort of. It was in another state. Leaving the town, and the farm, that day was the hardest thing. Galen drove in the rented moving van with Sarah riding shotgun, and I drove in the car loaded with pets. All the way along the road, she and Galen sang every worship song they could think of. I shut the door of the car and drove, without looking back. I didn't need to look to know what I would see, and I wondered if we would ever have any sort of stable life again.

We settled into the town and began attending a small, nondenominational church. We stayed there for about three years, hearing from several people in time that our stopover there was simply a stepping-stone on our journey. The words felt unpredictable to me, nomadic somehow. Life seemed nothing like the stability we had known at the farm. Before too long, we began to see stepping-stones present themselves.

A few months after our arrival, we learned that displaced farmers and oil field workers could be retrained for other occupations and could receive scholarships. After Galen graduated from a water technology program at a local college, a job presented itself. It was with American Water, a company that had holdings across the United States. He was offered a job in management because he had possessed a bachelor's degree. Galen had already obtained a degree in biology. After high school, he had not wanted to go to college, but preferred to stay and farm. His family had insisted on furthering his education. That new job would take us to the east coast. We would move many times during his career. One move led us back to the Midwest again. Galen retired from the water industry in 2019. But long before his planned retirement, we began planning on where we wanted to live. Our thoughts drifted naturally and easily back to the farm. Back home.

We began to formulate our plan to buy back the eight-acre parcel of land Galen's parents had sold the year we left town. On it were the farmhouse, a granary, and a small pen in which we had kept cattle and sheep when we lived there. We had understood the importance of someone living on the home place; but the fact that they had sold it had stung both of us. We guessed that no one had ever envisioned us coming back. We started out slowly, driving to the small town we had come from once or twice a month, plotting our move and saying nothing of our plans to anyone. To show you the depth of our devotion, we had gone as far as to develop what we called a two-year plan to recover the farmhouse and property. We were well into the second year of that two-year plan, a mere three months from realizing our dream, when we discovered that the farmhouse and land would not be for sale. We were not ready for that direction change.

Not dissuaded, we quickly regrouped with a strategy for building a home on a piece of property we still owned in the area, even considering the unplowed field behind the farmhouse. But somehow the excitement of our plans began to diminish. Problems soon developed in the guise of weather and access to the land. A long road would have to be constructed and a water well drilled. Other pieces of property were just as inaccessible to us due to the muddy, unpaved roads and the high snow load that would occur each winter, possibly leaving us stranded for long periods of time. Due to the decrease in population in the county, the roads were no longer maintained as they once had been. The list of negatives grew with each visit. Our focus had been on the home, and the move, but as we traveled back and forth, we began to see that things had changed. Things we had not accounted for when we had made our plans.

It had been over thirty years since we had left. The town had changed in our long absence; it had become smaller in some way, with fewer amenities than we had had before we left. Workmen and tradesmen necessary to build homes, or do repair work, were very few. Farming had continued to change, as well. There were nearly no small farms left in the area. Most of the people we had known, and whom Galen had grown up with, had left the area entirely. Or, if they had remained, their children had gone on due to lack of jobs in the area. But it would be the faces of those we saw on our trips back that told us the greatest story of change. They were strangers to us. Nothing had remained the same as it had been. Our wonderful pastor and teacher had long since died, and the small church we had once taught Sunday school in had never outgrown the tiny building it had occupied all those years ago. Galen's parents had both died, as had uncles and aunts and other distant relations who lived in the area. Though we loved the remoteness, the wide-open skies, and the solitude there on the Kansas prairie, we found ourselves feeling it less friendly, and incredibly lonely.

Our hearts had been so fixed on returning there for so very long, and we could not have imagined God not wanting us to go home. With our inability to purchase the farmhouse back, and the difficulties of building a new home, it seemed that our path was blocked, the door shut and padlocked. To be honest, we had no other plan in mind. A panic settled over us. It was at this time of complete chaos that we began to hear God speak to us, at last. This blocked opportunity was teaching us, though we had difficulty hearing or seeing it right away. Yes, we had our desires, our plans; but God continued to guide our steps. The door that had directed us away from our farm all those years ago remained closed to us. For a time, we seemed to feel the pain of it as intensely as we had the first time we left.

"You know," my wise husband said one day when we seemed to have reached an impasse with our dream, "*no* is a good answer, Amy."

Of course, he was right.

The stepping-stones would lead us to the small town in Missouri where we had first come when we left the farm. We purchased a home with acreage and began to sell the hay from our hay meadow. We did not make much money off the sale, but we were engaged in farming again!

There have always been articles written about the "what ifs" of life. I usually avoid them. I have read them before; the people were tragic as they ruminated about their regrets in life of opportunities not taken, life denying them their true destinies. And with the complaints came the words: "What if? What if? What if?" Two small words, with huge potential to bring grief into our hearts, make us discontented, and bring to us a longing for something we can no longer have. We cannot go back; we cannot turn time around to change the past. I do not even believe we can honestly imagine what might have been. I began to ponder on the ifs.

If we had remained in that small town, our daughters might not have met our sons-on-law.

If we hadn't had our sons-in-law, we would not have the grandchildren we have, right now, this moment.

If we had not left the farm, Galen would not have had the long and successful career he had in the water industry for over thirty years.

If we had not taken the job in the town in Missouri when we left the farm, we would not have made the friends that we now cherish.

If we had remained at the farm, we might never have met the pastors and teachers through the years who fed us, challenged us, disappointed us, hurt us, helped us grow.

If we had remained at the farm, we might not have known that God was leading us to something far better than if we had remained.

If we hadn't gone through any of this, we would never have realized that salvation is a lifelong experience, a progression of steps, of slips, of falls, of risings; all part of a daily walk of dependence upon Him.

I had to stop counting the ifs of our life, overwhelmed by God. What I discovered in reviewing just a few of the ifs of our life was that they had all been life-altering events in our family. I could not imagine life as it could have been or might have been. There was no comparison between the what-ifs and our lives as we experienced them. God had ordained all our steps.

I recall the day when Galen's job in the oil field had ended. I wandered up the lane at the back of the property to the top of the hill. I stood there alone, staring out at the unplowed sod pasture. I wondered what would happen to us. Our lives were about to change. We would have to break out the ground of our lives, plant and cultivate, and see what might grow—if anything. I really did not know. But God did.

"Don't look back, because you are not going in that direction. Concentrate on what's ahead."

Those words, spoken all those years ago, still ring true today. That, and a scripture I read the other day. It is found in the book of Exodus:

> The LORD replied, "My Presence will go with you, and I will give you rest." Then Moses said to him, "If your Presence does not go with us, do not send us up from here." (Exodus 33:14–15 NIV)

Moses stated he was not going anywhere if God was not in the lead. We have come to understand that only too well. When the path in our lives has seemed most uncertain, He has been there. Not as a pillar of fire at night, nor a cloud of smoke during the day, as Moses witnessed, but there just the same. He came to us in stepping-stones and led us to our little farm in the Ozarks. All our steps mattered— even the most painful ones. The blessings of the Lord, His faithfulness toward us, His ever-present guidance, His protection over our lives have always reached out to us. Though we could not hear His voice at times, nor see His path because of our own tears or fixed desires, He was there, gently guiding us back home to Himself.

Every day is a choice for us all. And we are going His way.

Epilogue

I stared at the blank screen before me.

"Well." I said that out loud. I knew this because my dog, a Pembroke Welsh corgi named Wynne, padded into the room and stared at me.

"Ah—writer's block," her eyes seem to say to me.

"No, not really," I defended myself. Again, I had responded aloud, but I knew it this time. "Sometimes, it's just difficult."

Wynne looked at me for a time and then came near the desk, which flanked the window, to look at what I had thought was the usual squirrel or bird who had trespassed on her turf. But no. Her eyes were transfixed on the blank computer screen. What had she seen? It was then that I saw it too: my own reflection gazing back at me.

God had visited me that day in the guise of a blank screen, a clean slate, ready to continue to write His story of my life on my heart and in my mind. That had been His answer to my questioning. Once we see ourselves as we truly are, we realize we will always need the journey. It is not always without pain, but it is part of the process. We do not get anywhere on our own. It is God who calls us and directs our steps along the way. Every day I will behold a blank screen with the reflection of me and prepare for God to continue to write His story on my heart and in my life. Experiences change us, reveal our flaws, offer solutions, bring repentance and forgiveness and love, introduce us into a deeper relation with God. We grow and change. We stoop; we discover; we understand; we receive instruction; we move in another direction. At times, the experiences will be filled with purpose, at others disjointed, with no visible pattern discernable. People weave in and out of my life; situations come up, bringing with them sadness, joy, or confusion. And almost never is there a level path—not a consistent one, at any rate. We do not look like we did yesterday, nor will we look the same tomorrow. Change. That is what the journey is all about.

I reached toward the bookshelf in the den and picked up Momma's bright pink Bible. I smiled at the color, and I flipped through it, looking at her favorite scriptures, which she had underlined in pencil. I noticed a piece of paper clipped from a magazine and Scotch-taped to the inside of the back cover. I do not know who wrote it, but I understood it more at that moment, sitting before that blank screen:

> God is not so much interested in whether we reach our destination as in how we get there. To us arrival is everything, but to God the journey is the most important, for it is in the journey that we are perfected; and it is in the hardships that He is glorified as we trust Him.

Maybe you have been on some of these roads on your journey:

Roads that are filled with potholes and other obstacles.

Roads that did not resemble roads at all but trails, made to walk alone.

Winding, narrow roads that have no guardrails. (Yikes!)

Roads that are hidden in a heavy darkness, the way through revealed only a step at a time.

Roads that seem abandoned, lonely, and foreboding—the sort of roads we wish we could avoid.

Yet they all must be navigated. Take courage! We have an outstanding Navigator!

The blank screen seems to want to speak to me. It's time to continue my journey.

Off I go.

Notes

Preface

1   David E. Garland and Diana R. Garland, *Flawed Families of the Bible: How God's Grace Works through Imperfect Relationships* (Baker Publishing Group, 2007), 26–27.

Chapter 1: Hannibal

1   Charles Haddon Spurgeon, "Isaiah 64," in *Spurgeon's Verse Expositions of the Bible,* https://www.studylight.org/commentaries/spe/isaiah-64.html.
2   2 Kings 6:16–17.

Chapter 2: Mentor

1   Adela Rogers St. Johns, "Words to Grow On," *Guideposts,* July 19, 2012, https://www.guideposts.org/better-living/life-advice/finding-life-purpose/words-to-grow-on.

Chapter 4: The Search

1   Oswald Chambers, *My Utmost for His Highest,* April 3, edited by James Reimann, Discovery House Publishers, 1992.
    Portions of this article were previously published in *Virtue Magazine,* Volume 7, Number 5, January/February 1985, *One Woman's Journal,* Amy Mahan Robbins, *The Gathering Place.*

Chapter 5: The Swimsuit

1   p. 196–197, C. S. Lewis, *Mere Christianity*, Harper One (Harper Collins Publishers), 2001.
(227 pages)

Chapter 6: The Message

1   Oswald Chambers, *My Utmost for His Highest*, Nov 7, edited by James Reimann, Discovery House Publishers, 1992.

Chapter 7: The Bullfrog and the Tractor

1   Oswald Chambers, *My Utmost for His Highest*, November 14, edited by James Reimann, Discovery House Publishers, 1992.
2   p.232, *Webster's New Collegiate Dictionary*, G. C. Merriam Company, 1975. (1534 pages)

Chapter 8: The Woman on the Sofa

1   p. 39, Exodus 3.5, *The Rational Bible*, Exodus, Dennis Prager, 2018 Regenery Publishing (520 pages)

Chapter 9: The Dream

1   p. 83 [1114] Corrie Ten Boom, *Topical Encyclopedia of Living Quotations*, Edited by Sherwood Elliot Wirt and Kersten Beckstrom, Bethany House Publishers, 1982. (290 pages)

Chapter 11: The Right Stuff

1   p. 21, *The Right Stuff*, Tom Wolfe, Macmillian, 2008. (448 pages)

Chapter 12: Broken

1   p. 5 [58], Charles G. Colton *Topical Encyclopedia of Living Quotations*, Edited by Sherwood Elliot Wirt and Kersten Beckstrom, Bethany House Publishers, 1982. (290 pages)
Recommended reading:
The Subtle Power of Spiritual Abuse, David Johnson and Jeff Van Vonderren, Bethany House Publishing, Minneapolis, 1991 (234 pages).
*All names in this article have been changed to protect their privacy.

Chapter 15: The Unplowed Field

1   Frederick W. Faber p.87[1166] *Topical Encyclopedia of Living Quotations*, Edited by Sherwood Elliot Wirt and Kersten Beckstrom, Bethany House Publishers, 1982. (290 pages)

2   Ecclesiastes 3:1–8

Printed in the United States
by Baker & Taylor Publisher Services